AN INTRODUCTION TO
JIG AND TOOL DESIGN

THE TECHNICAL COLLEGE SERIES

General editor

E. G. STERLAND

J.P., M.A., B.Sc.(Eng), F.I.Mech.E., F.R.Ae.S.
Principal, Rolls-Royce Technical College, Bristol

by the same author
Introduction to Workshop Technology
Materials for Engineers

AN INTRODUCTION TO
JIG AND TOOL DESIGN

M. H. A. KEMPSTER

C.Eng., M.I.Mech.E., A.F.R.Ae.S.,
M.I.Prod.E.

Senior Lecturer in Production Technology
Rolls-Royce Technical College

HODDER AND STOUGHTON
LONDON SYDNEY AUCKLAND TORONTO

ISBN 0 340 18221 0

First published 1964
Second edition 1968
Third edition 1974

Reprinted 1975, 1976, 1978, 1980, 1981, 1982

Printed in Great Britain for Hodder and Stoughton
Educational, a division of Hodder and Stoughton Ltd,
Mill Road, Dunton Green, Sevenoaks, Kent by
Brown Knight & Truscott Ltd, London and Tonbridge.

GENERAL EDITOR'S FOREWORD

The Technical College Series covers a wide range of technician and craft courses, and includes books designed to cover subjects in National Certificate and Diploma courses, and City and Guilds Technician and Craft syllabuses. This important sector of technical education has been the subject of very considerable changes over the past few years. The more recent of these have been the result of the establishment of the Training Boards, under the Industrial Training Act. Although the Boards have no direct responsibility for education, their activities in ensuring proper training in industry have had a marked influence on the complementary courses which technical colleges must provide. For example, the introduction of the module system of training for craftsmen by the Engineering Industry Training Board led directly to the City and Guilds 500 series of courses.

The Haslegrave Committee on Technician Courses and Examinations reported late in 1969, and made recommendations for far-reaching administrative changes, which will undoubtedly eventually result in new syllabuses and examination requirements.

It should, perhaps, be emphasised that these changes are being made not for their own sake, but to meet the needs of industry and the young men and women who are seeking to equip themselves for a career in industry. And industry and technology are changing at an unprecedented rate, so that technical education must be more concerned with fundamental principles than with techniques.

Many of the books in the Technical College Series are now standard works, having stood the test of time over a long period of years. To keep pace with the rapid changes taking place both in courses and in technology, new works and new editions are constantly being added to the list. The Publishers are fully aware of the part that well-written up-to-date textbooks can play in supplementing teaching, and it is their intention that the Technical College Series shall continue to make a substantial contribution to the development of technical education.

E. G. Sterland

PREFACE

The design of jigs and tools is important because the rate of production and the quality of the work produced by machine tools and presses can only be as good as the cutting tools, press tools and holding equipment will allow.

The author assumes that the reader has a sound knowledge of basic machine tools and processes, and aims at the application of this knowledge to the design of production equipment with due regard to economics.

In this book, principles of jig and tool design are presented without excessive text, and without duplication of topics normally included in books on Manufacturing Technology and Engineering Drawing; it is therefore suitable for students following a TEC programme.

The reader is reminded that a subject can only be learned by active participation, and this is particularly true of design. Production equipment designs should therefore be examined, and the good and bad features of each identified. This should be followed by the preparation of as many original designs as possible, which should be critically examined by a competent designer. These designs should preferably be drawn actual size so that a clear idea of hand and swarf clearances, and of the size and weight of the parts is obtained; and should include freehand work to avoid waste of time.

The author wishes to thank his wife, who generally assisted in the preparation of the book.

M. H. A. KEMPSTER

CONTENTS

CHAPTER I

INTRODUCTION

1.10. Production equipment

Jigs and fixtures are provided to convert standard machine tools into specialised machine tools. They are usually associated with large-scale production by semi-skilled operators, but they are also used for small-scale production when interchangeability is important, and by skilled machinists when the workpiece is difficult to hold without special equipment. Limit gauges are used when acceptance or rejection is required rather than actual measurement, and inspection fixtures are used when the positions of holes and faces, etc., are to be checked. Assembly and welding fixtures are provided to hold parts so that the operator will have both hands free. Special tools are used when complicated shapes are to be machined. 1.11. Jigs are machine shop devices that include means of tool guiding; they are only applicable to operations performed on a drilling machine. Fixtures are holding devices that do not include means of tool guiding, but they may include means of setting the cutter; fixtures are used for milling, turning, grinding and similar operations.

1.20. The economics approach to the provision of special equipment

If the cost of the equipment is important, the allowable cost must usually be related to the reduction in cost as a result of using the equipment, and to the quantity of workpieces to be produced. The minimum quantity to be produced to permit a given expenditure is known as the *breakeven quantity* (Q).

$$Q = \frac{X}{A - B}$$

Where $X =$ cost of the equipment;

$\quad\quad A =$ cost to produce one off without the proposed equipment;

$\quad\quad B =$ cost to produce one off with the proposed equipment.

1.21. Special equipment is sometimes provided for small-quantity production if interchangeability is demanded, or if the workpiece is difficult to hold; the cost of the equipment must then be related to the value of the operation.

The design of jigs and fixtures

1.30. The first step in the design is to draw the outline of the workpiece (usually in red) in the required position for the machining, and to draw the *location system* and the *clamping system*. The *tool guiding* or the *tool setting* system is then drawn in, and finally these features are linked together to form a unit. The general principles of design are listed in this chapter; the principles of location and clamping, and the features associated with the more common jigs and fixtures are discussed in the following chapters. The general arrangement drawing of the equipment should have a title block that includes the reference number of the equipment, the part number and description of the workpiece, and details of the operation for which the equipment is to be used. The arrangement drawing should also include a parts list containing a description and information regarding the material, treatment and quantity of each detail; these parts should be identified on the arrangement by balloon reference.

1.31. PRINCIPLES OF JIG AND FIXTURE DESIGN

1.311. *Location*

1. Ensure that the workpiece is given the desired constraint.
2. Position the locators so that swarf will not cause mal-alignment.
3. Make the location points adjustable if a rough casting or a forging is being machined.
4. Introduce foolproofing devices such as fouling pins, projections, etc., to prevent incorrect positioning of the workpiece.
5. Make all location points visible to the operator from his working position.
6. Make the location progressive (i.e. locate on one locator and then on to the other).

1.312. *Clamping*

1. Position the clamps to give best resistance to the cutting forces.
2. Position the clamps so that they do not cause deformation of the workpiece.
3. If possible, make the clamps integral with the fixture body.
4. Make all clamping and location motions easy and natural to perform.

1.313. *Clearance*

1. Allow ample clearance to allow for variation of workpiece size.
2. Allow ample clearance for the operator's hands.
3. Ensure that there is ample swarf clearance, and clearance to

enable the workpiece to be removed after machining, when burrs will be present.

1.314. *Stability and Rigidity*

1. Provide four feet so that uneven seating will be obvious, and ensure that the forces on the equipment act within the area enclosed by a line joining the seating points.
2. Make the equipment as rigid as is necessary for the operation.
3. Provide means of positioning and bolting the equipment to the machine table or spindle if required.

1.315. *Handling*

1. Make the equipment as light as possible, and easy to handle; ensure that no sharp corners are present, and provide lifting points if it is heavy.

1.316. *General*

1. Keep the design simple in order to minimise cost, and to avoid breakdown caused by over-complication.
2. Utilise standard and proprietary parts as much as possible.
3. Check that the workpiece can be loaded into, and removed from the equipment; the design technique whereby the equipment is designed around the workpiece, tends to make this a common source of error.

1.32. CONSTRUCTION METHODS AND MATERIALS USED

Jigs and fixtures may be cast in iron, fabricated from steel plates and machined parts by welding, or built-up by bolting sections and machined parts together. The method used will depend upon the size and shape of the equipment, and upon the time available to manufacture it. Location faces, unless particularly large, are made from surface-hardened steel, and attached to the base. Knobs and handles are often made from plastics materials, and assembly fixtures in glass-fibre are sometimes produced using the wet lay-up method.

1.321. Modern practice makes extensive use of proprietary bases, clamp plates, nuts, handles, tenons, etc., and also of standard press tool parts.

The function and organisation of the jig office

1.40. The Jig Office is usually responsible for the preparation of raw material (casting and forging) drawings, for the design and detail drawings of tooling equipment, and for the issue of drawings and instructions for their manufacture. It works in conjunction with the Planning Office, and often these two offices are combined to form one department. The Jig Office is usually headed by a Chief Draughtsman, and is divided up into sections; these sections are usually run by a Section Leader, who is responsible for a particular product, or for the 'tooling up' of a group of machines; this specialisation ensures that experience of previous similar work can be readily utilised. When a product is to be tooled up urgently, the services of a Contract Tool Drawing Office is often obtained in order to avoid the temporary employment of designers and draughtsmen; these offices charge a fee for the tooling up of a complete component, or for each design produced; alternatively they will supply staff to work in the overloaded office. In addition to the technical staff, the Jig Office employs clerical staff to maintain records of equipment, issue and modifications to drawings, and to deal with purchasing arrangements; a print room is usually attached to the office.

CHAPTER 2

PLANNING

2.10. Machine shop process planning

The object of planning is to determine the most economical method of producing a particular component; the equipment that is available must be taken into account, and so the method selected may need to be a compromise.

2.11. Planning is usually done some time before machining is due to commence so that (1) the raw material dimensions can be settled, (2) the machine tool requirements can be assessed, (3) the jigs, fixtures, tools and gauges can be designed and manufactured, (4) the labour requirements can be studied, (5) an accurate estimate of the time taken to machine the component can be made.

2.12. The machining sequence will depend upon the size of the machine shop, and the class of labour and machines that are available.

The amount of detail contained on the process sheet will be only small if the planning is for a tool room or similar machine shop, but if the planning is for a production shop, the process will be very detailed. When the planning is for a production shop, drawings are often made showing the machining dimensions for each operation; these drawings are used for the intermediate inspection operations, and the 'master drawing' only used for the final inspection.

2.20. Choice of equipment and method

Centre lathes are associated with small-scale production, and with skilled machinists; parts produced on a centre lathe will not need to be finished by grinding unless the tolerances are extremely fine, or if the part is to be hardened, and will need to be ground afterwards to remove distortion due to the quenching. Turret lathes and capstan lathes are associated with larger-scale production and with semi-skilled machinists; parts so produced will need to be finished by grinding unless the tolerances are coarse.

2.21. Universal milling machines are associated with tool room work; horizontal and vertical column-and-knee machines and fixed bed machines are used for production work. Similarly, universal grinding machines are associated with tool room work, and internal and external grinding machines with production work.

2.22. Marking out for machining is only used for very small quantities, but may be speeded up by the use of templates; jigs and fixtures are used for large-scale production. A dividing head is used for spacing when small quantities are involved, and indexing jigs and fixtures used for larger quantities.

2.23. The following tables shows some of the differences between the methods used in the tool room and those used in a production shop.

Tool room	Production shop
Castings and forgings are marked out	Marking out only used for 'trial' material
Work located by 'setting up' using a dial indicator	Work located in jigs and fixtures
Work held in a vice, clamped to machine table, in a chuck or on a stump that is turned by the machinist	Work located and held in special vice jaws, in a fixture or special collet, etc.
Turning done on a centre lathe	Turning done on a capstan lathe or turret lathe
Grinding done when tolerances are fine, or after heat-treatment	Extensive use of grinding because unless tolerances are wide, other methods of machining by semi-skilled machinists will not produce the required accuracy
Circular table used for many profiling operations	Profile plates used extensively
Dividing head used for spacing of holes, etc.	Indexing jigs and fixtures used for spacing
Awkward shapes finished by filing	All shapes machined (if not 'as cast')

Although the method adopted for the production shop will be different from that for the tool room, the differences will be mainly of detail and the precise equipment. The fundamental methods themselves will not be very different, and the method used for production can be regarded as a variation to suit the particular requirements of production.

2.30. Planning method

Planning must be methodical because its purpose is to produce method; if the following procedure is adopted, the work of process planning will be simplified and be more effective.

1. Study the component drawing in order to understand the duty of the component so that the relative importance of its features can be determined; this study will show if tolerances on dimensions are applied to produce desired fits, or to ensure clearance between the part and other parts upon assembly. As a result of this study, the planner should also be familiar with the shape, size and weight of the part, and know if it is likely to produce balancing problems.

2. List, or ring the dimensions of features that are to be machined, indicate if roughing, followed by finishing, will be required; also indicate the important dimensions, with a view to considering which are to be used for location purposes.

3. Prepare a rough draft process with due regard to the following basic rules:

   (a) Establish **at least** one datum at the first opportunity; for example, face the end when turning, or face a large surface when milling. It is often possible to produce a second datum at the same time, e.g. a bore that is square with the end face.

   (b) Produce as much as possible from one setting; it must be realised that every new setting reduces the possibility of accuracy, because machining tolerances must be allowed both on the workpiece and on the jig and fixture parts, and also upon the machine tool itself.

   (c) In order to ensure very accurate relationship between the features, the original datum features must be used as long as possible; when they can no longer be used (for example, when they themselves are finish-machined), the locations then used must have been machined when locating from the original ones.

   (d) Group similar operations together if possible (for example, make drilling operations follow each other). This will reduce handling times, and assist the progress department.

   (e) Perform accurate operations (for example, grinding), at the end of the machining sequence so that damage to important surfaces is minimised. NOTE: a feature may have material left on for finishing, and still be used for location, provided that it is machined sufficiently accurately.

   (f) Introduce inspection operations at strategic stages to avoid scrap, and wasted effort upon incorrectly machined parts.

   (g) Introduce a burr-removal operation before a feature is used for location.

   (h) Ensure that all features are position-controlled.

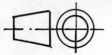

DIMS IN
MM.

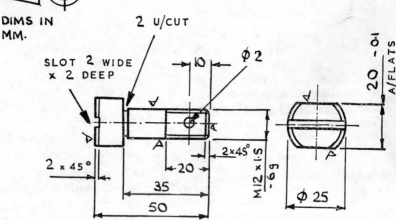

FIG 2.1 **SPECIAL BOLT**

MAKE FROM 25 DIA STEEL BAR
MACHINE AT '√'

Operation layout for special bolt

Operation number	Description	Machine
1	In collet: face end, turn shank diameter 12 mm − 0·2 mm for location. Form undercut and shoulder. Chamfer end and screw to length. Part off to length + 1 mm.	Capstan lathe
2	Reverse. In collet; face end and chamfer	Capstan lathe
3	View	View bench
4	In fixture: locating from shank. Gang mill flats and slot	Horizontal mill
5	Remove burrs	Burr bench
6	In jig: locating from shank and one flat. Drill 2 mm dia. hole in shank	Sensitive drill
7	Remove burrs from hole	Burr bench
8	Final view	View bench

8

4. Check the draft process to ensure that all machining is called up, and then finalise the process.

Specimen operation layouts

2.40. The following two operation layouts will illustrate planning techniques; these examples do not include heat-treatment operations, but when hardening is done, it is usually followed by grinding to remove distortion due to quenching.

OPERATION LAYOUT FOR SPECIAL BOLT (page 8)

2.41. In this example the shank is made more accurately than is demanded by the drawing because it is to be used as a location. The workpiece is symmetrical about the shank axis until the head is milled, or the shank is drilled; it follows then, that the first of these features to be machined becomes the second locator, and will be used to control the rotational position of the part about the shank axis. The hole in the shank is unsuitable as a location feature because it is very small, and because it would demand a retractable locator; the slot in the head is obviously unsuitable, but **one** of the flats can be used with the shank (only one flat must be used for location, because two flats and the shank would together produce redundant location; see Chapter 3, paragraph 3.40). The burrs caused by milling must be removed before the head can be used for location.

OPERATION LAYOUT FOR FULCRUM PIN (page 10)

2.42. In this example the stem is eccentric relative to the flange and the spigot; the spigot is therefore the main location feature, and is machined first. The second locator (the 12 mm diameter hole) is machined directly after the spigot, to produce a rotational locator about the spigot axis; it is therefore necessary to introduce a drilling operation between the turning operations (operations 1 and 3). When the 12 mm diameter hole is produced (at operation 2) the 10 mm diameter holes and their spotfaces are also produced. The spigot and the 12 mm diameter hole are used together as location for all the machining operations that follow except for the operation at which the spigot itself is finish-machined (operation 8). It is necessary that the spigot and the stem are finished by grinding because turning using production techniques will not produce the required accuracy. It will be seen that the flange profile is used for location about the spigot axis until the 12 mm diameter hole is machined.

Operation layout for fulcrum pin (see fig. 2.2 on page 11)

Operation number	Description	Machine
1	In fixture—locate from flange profile. Face spigot end, drill 10 mm dia. to depth, chamfer and turn spigot dia. 48·4 mm dia. — 0·02 mm for location	Turret lathe
2	View	View bench
3	Reverse: In jig, locate from spigot and flange profile. Drill and spotface 4 holes 10 mm dia. Drill and ream 12 mm dia. hole	Radial drill
4	Remove burrs	Burr bench
5	In fixture: locate from spigot and 12 mm dia. hole. Face, drill and tap hole in stem. Chamfer and turn relief diameter and 25·40 mm — 0·02 mm stem dia. Face boss to 25·2 mm ± 0·1 mm for location and form undercut	Turret lathe
6	View	View bench
7	In jig: locate from spigot and 12 mm dia. hole. Drill 2 holes 3 mm dia.	Sensitive drill
8	In fixture: locate from stem and 12 mm dia. hole. Finish grind spigot and flange face	External grinder
9	Reverse: In fixture, locate from spigot and 12 mm dia. hole. Finish grind stem dia. and boss face	External grinder
10	Remove burrs	Burr bench
11	Final view	View bench

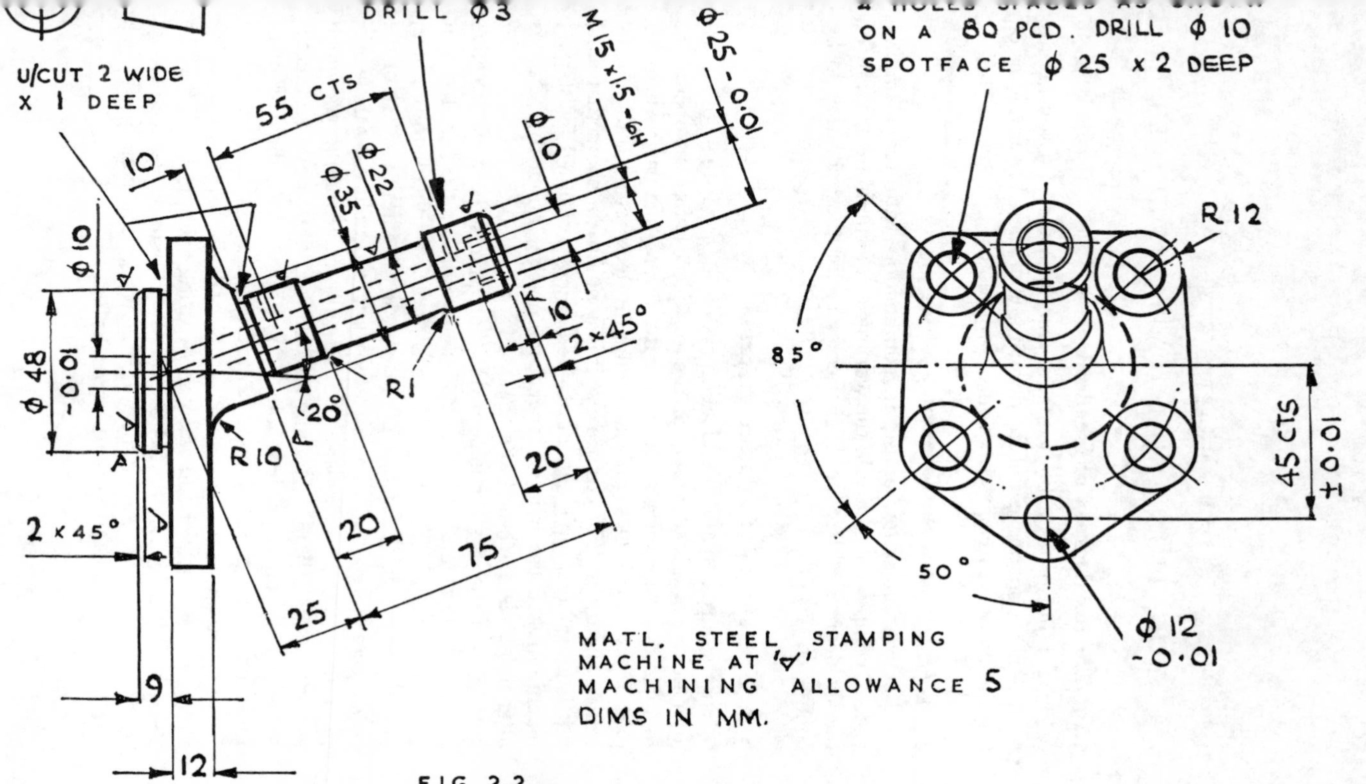

FULCRUM PIN

FIG 2.2

MATL. STEEL STAMPING
MACHINE AT ∇.
MACHINING ALLOWANCE 5
DIMS IN MM.

CHAPTER 3

LOCATION AND LOCATION DEVICES

3.10. The six degrees of freedom

Fig. 3.1 illustrates a body that is free in space. A body in this condition has six degrees of freedom; three of these are freedoms of translation and three are freedoms of rotation.

3.20. The duty of the location system

The location system must, in conjunction with the clamping system, completely constrain the workpiece, or eliminate as many of the six degrees of freedom as is necessary for the operation to be completed with the required accuracy.

3.30. The choice of location system

The requirements of the location system depend upon the operation being performed, and upon the workpiece before the operation. Fig. 3.2 illustrates three stages in the machining of a part; when this part is positioned for stage 2 machining it does not need to be controlled about the XX axis because it is symmetrical about that axis, but it must be completely constrained when positioned for stage 3 machining because it is no longer symmetrical about the XX axis after hole A is machined at stage 2.

3.31. When there is a choice of location points the most effective location system must be selected. The cylinder is the best location shape because a cylindrical locator is the least difficult to produce, and because a single locator of this shape will eliminate five of the six degrees of freedom. The ease of loading and unloading the workpiece must also be considered. This is illustrated in fig. 3.3 which shows two methods of machining a workpiece; at operation 2 there is a choice between machining hole 'L' and hole 'H'. As the workpiece must be constrained when it is positioned for operation 3, two locators are necessary. If method 'A' is used, the locators for operation 3 will be parallel and easily seen during loading, but if method 'B' is used, the locator that engages hole 'H' will not be seen easily, and must be retractable so that the workpiece can be loaded. Method 'A' is obviously the better method.

LOCATION

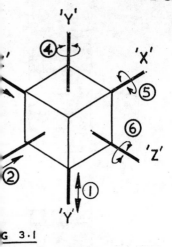

FIG 3.1

CONSIDER THE POSSIBLE MOVEMENTS OF THE FREE BODY SHOWN, WITH RESPECT TO THE THREE MUTUALLY PERPENDICULAR AXES 'X-X', 'Y-Y', & 'Z-Z'.

IT CAN :-

1. MOVE ALONG 'Y-Y'
2. MOVE ALONG 'X-X'
3. MOVE ALONG 'Z-Z'

THREE FREEDOMS OF TRANSLATION

4. ROTATE ABOUT 'Y-Y'
5. ROTATE ABOUT 'X-X'
6. ROTATE ABOUT 'Z-Z'

THREE FREEDOMS OF ROTATION

TOTAL:- SIX DEGREES OF FREEDOM

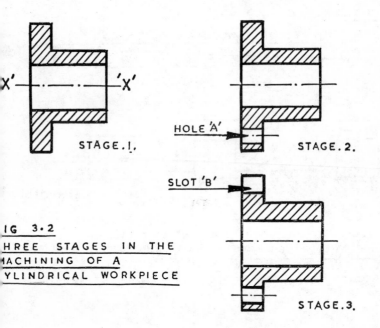

FIG 3.2
THREE STAGES IN THE MACHINING OF A CYLINDRICAL WORKPIECE

13

LOCATION

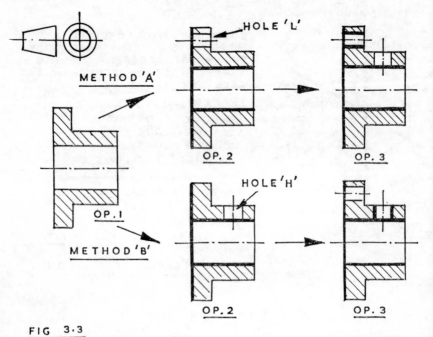

METHOD 'A'

HOLE 'L'

OP. 2

OP. 3

OP.1

METHOD 'B'

HOLE 'H'

OP. 2

OP. 3

FIG 3.3

TWO METHODS OF MACHINING A WORKPIECE

(LOCATIONS SHOWN BY HEAVY LINES)

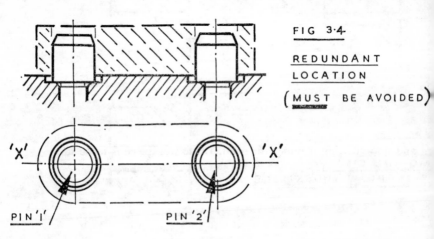

FIG 3.4

REDUNDANT LOCATION

(MUST BE AVOIDED)

'X'   'X'

PIN '1'   PIN '2'

3.40. Redundant location

A redundant location is said to exist when two locators are attempting to constrain one freedom from two location points; it must be avoided. Fig. 3.4 illustrates a location system in which the workpiece is located over two pins; the purpose of pin 2 is to prevent rotation about pin 1 but the system is such that both pins are attempting to constrain the workpiece along XX, and so redundant location is introduced. This system is quite impractical because workpieces would only be accepted by the location system if the workpieces and location system were *without error* (the correct solution to this problem is shown on page 22). Redundant location will also occur if a workpiece is located from two concentric cylinders, or between two fixed vee locations.

3.50. The six point location principle

This principle is illustrated in fig. 3.5. Six pads and clamping system as shown, or a system of location and clamping that produces the same effect is necessary to produce complete constraint.

Locators

3.60. Locators are usually made separate from the fixture or jig body, and are of direct or casehardened steel accurately ground to size (to give a slight clearance fit in the case of cylindrical location) and accurately positioned in the jig or fixture body.

Locators may be classified as (*a*) flat, (*b*) cylindrical, (*c*) conical, (*d*) vee; they may be fixed or adjustable according to the circumstances.

3.70. Typical locators

PAGE 17. LOCATORS THAT CONTROL THE WORKPIECE FROM FLAT SURFACES OR FROM ITS PROFILE BY MEANS OF PADS OR PINS

3.71. Fig. 3.6 shows a simple support pad as used to position or support the workpiece from a flat surface; it is an interference fit in the base, and good seating is ensured by chamfering its location hole and undercutting it under the head. If the workpiece is to be supported from more than one face in a given plane, adjustment must be provided for the pads and pins at the additional faces; fig. 3.7 illustrates a simple adjustable pin, but more elaborate systems are used for remote adjustment (see fig. 3.8). Figs. 3.9 and 3.10 illustrate pins used for simple location from a profile.

THE SIX-POINT LOCATION PRINCIPLE

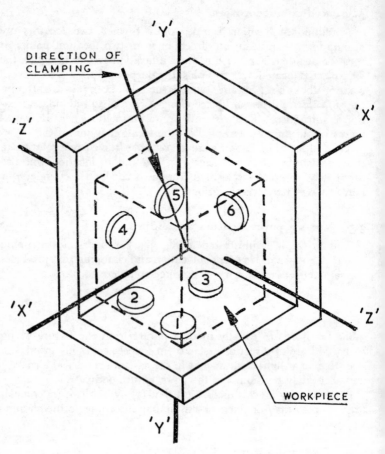

IN CONJUNCTION WITH THE CLAMPING SYSTEM :-

PADS 1, 2, & 3   CONSTRAIN WORKPIECE ALONG 'Y-Y', ABOUT 'Z-Z', AND ABOUT 'X-X'.

PADS 4 & 5   CONSTRAIN WORKPIECE ALONG 'Z-Z', AND ABOUT 'Y-Y'.

PAD 6   CONSTRAINS WORKPIECE ALONG 'X-X'

THE WORKPIECE IS THEREFORE FULLY CONSTRAINED

FIG 3.5

LOCATORS

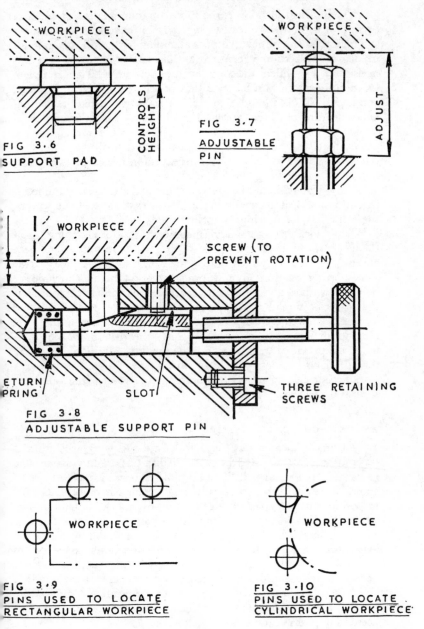

FIG 3.6
SUPPORT PAD

CONTROLS HEIGHT

FIG 3.7
ADJUSTABLE PIN

ADJUST

WORKPIECE

SCREW (TO PREVENT ROTATION)

RETURN SPRING

SLOT

THREE RETAINING SCREWS

FIG 3.8
ADJUSTABLE SUPPORT PIN

WORKPIECE

FIG 3.9
PINS USED TO LOCATE RECTANGULAR WORKPIECE

WORKPIECE

FIG 3.10
PINS USED TO LOCATE CYLINDRICAL WORKPIECE

17

PAGE 20. LOCATION FROM CYLINDRICAL SURFACES

3.72. Cylindrical location is the most common method of location because it is the most effective. Fig. 3.11 on page 20 shows a short cylindrical locator which, with the clamping force, will constrain all six degrees of freedom excepting that of rotation about its own axis (axis YY), for which a second locator must be used for complete location. Locators must be accurately positioned relative to the base, and kept as short as possible to prevent 'binding' during the loading and unloading of the workpiece. If a long locator must be employed to give greater support to a weak workpiece, location must only take place at the extreme ends of the locator, and so the post must be relieved as shown in fig. 3.11(a). Large locators are usually lightened by boring a hole along the YY axis.

Location posts should be given a generous lead to facilitate loading, and should sit in a recess in the base so that dirt will not prevent the workpiece from being correctly seated (see fig. 3.11).

When a location post is used in conjunction with clamping (as in the jig shown in fig. 5.13 on page 41) it must be secured to the base otherwise it may be pulled out by the clamping force. Fig. 3.11(b) shows locator retention by nut; other retention methods include set bolt and washer, and flange and set screws. It must be emphasised that a screw thread will not position the locator axis, and if the locator is screwed directly into the base a location diameter must be incorporated in addition to the screw (the drill bush shown in fig. 5.7 is provided with a location diameter in addition to a screw thread). The location pot shown in fig. 3.12 is used to locate a workpiece from a spigot or shaft diameter; it produces the same constraints as a location post.

PAGE 21. CONICAL LOCATION

3.73. Conical locators are used to locate the workpiece from a tapered hole or shaft, and when applied in this manner are similar to location posts and pots. The examples shown on page 21 are of conical location from cylindrical holes or shafts where it is necessary to position the workpiece from the axis of the location feature, but where the diameter of the feature is not particularly accurate. The examples shown in figs. 3.13 are effective unless the height of the workpiece is to be controlled. When conical location is to be used to position a drill or profile-milling plate which must be a fixed height above the base an adjustable conical locator (fig. 3.14) is used; it will be seen that the screwed locator must be position-controlled by means of a location diameter, because the screw thread will not accurately position the axis of the locator.

PAGE 22. CYLINDRICAL LOCATORS IN COMBINATION

3.74. It has already been stated that a cylindrical locator will constrain five degrees of freedom; when complete constraint is required
a second locator is necessary. When the two location features are of
different sizes the larger is located by the principal locator, which
constrains five freedoms, and the second locator is used only to constrain the remaining freedom; the principal locator is usually the
longer so that the workpiece can be located on it and then rotated
until engaged with the second locator. When the second locator is
to engage with a cylindrical location feature, particular care must
be taken to avoid redundant location. Fig. 3.15, shown actual
size, illustrates location from two holes; in this arrangement the
second locator is shaped as shown in fig. 3.15(a) so that it will only
influence the position of the workpiece along AA. When several holes
are suitable for use as second location point, a hole that is as far
away as possible from the principal locator is selected in order to
minimise the angular error caused by error of workpiece or locator
(see fig. 13.16).

PAGES 23 & 24. VEE LOCATION

3.75. Vee locators are used to locate from cylindrical or part
cylindrical profiles; they may be fixed or sliding, but in both systems
their position must be controlled. Two fixed vee locators may be
used for reasonably accurate location from an accurate profile or
for rough location; a system of one fixed and one sliding locator is
used for more accurate location. A sliding locator, or in some cases
a fixed locator, is used in conjunction with a principal cylindrical
locator. When a vee location system includes a sliding vee a small
downward clamping force can be introduced by inclining the sides
of the vee as shown in fig. 3.19. When vee location is employed, care
must be taken to ensure that it will control the workpiece in the
required direction (see figs. 3.21).

LOCATORS

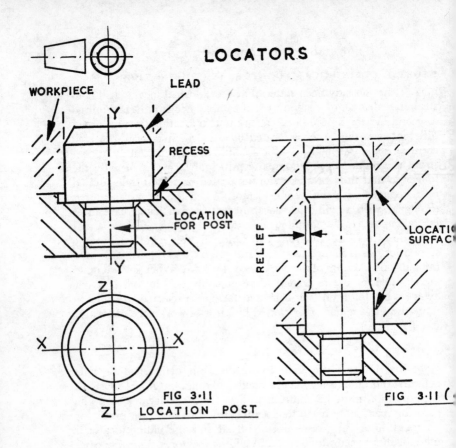

WORKPIECE

LEAD

RECESS

LOCATION FOR POST

Y

Y

Z

X — X

Z

FIG 3·11
LOCATION POST

RELIEF

LOCATIO
SURFAC

FIG 3·11 (

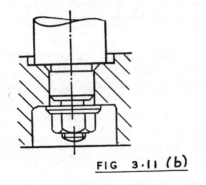

FIG 3·11 (b)

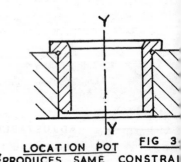

Y

Y

LOCATION POT
(PRODUCES SAME CONSTRAI
AS LOCATION POST)

FIG 3

LOCATORS

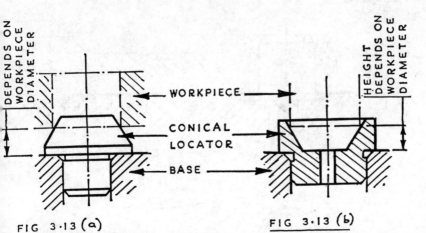

FIG 3.13 (a)   FIG 3.13 (b)

FIXED CONICAL LOCATORS

LOCATE WORKPIECE FROM AXIS OF HOLE OR
SHAFT, BUT HEIGHT DEPENDS UPON DIAMETER

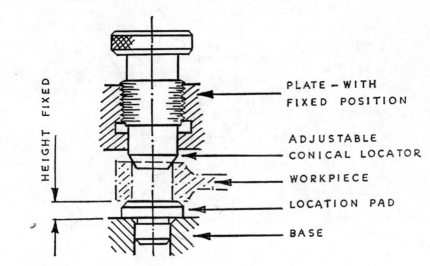

FIG 3.14   **ADJUSTABLE CONICAL LOCATOR**

WITH LOCATION PAD WILL LOCATE WORKPIECE
FROM AXIS OF HOLE OR SHAFT, AND CONTROL
HEIGHT ABOVE BASE

LOCATORS

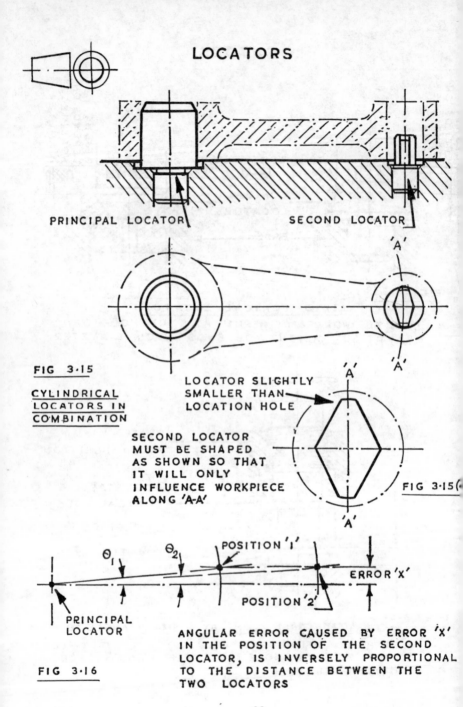

PRINCIPAL LOCATOR

SECOND LOCATOR

'A'

FIG 3·15

CYLINDRICAL
LOCATORS IN
COMBINATION

LOCATOR SLIGHTLY
SMALLER THAN
LOCATION HOLE

'A'

'A'

SECOND LOCATOR
MUST BE SHAPED
AS SHOWN SO THAT
IT WILL ONLY
INFLUENCE WORKPIECE
ALONG 'A-A'

FIG 3·15(·

'A'

Θ_1 Θ_2 POSITION '1'

ERROR 'x'

POSITION '2'

PRINCIPAL
LOCATOR

ANGULAR ERROR CAUSED BY ERROR 'x'
IN THE POSITION OF THE SECOND
LOCATOR, IS INVERSELY PROPORTIONAL
TO THE DISTANCE BETWEEN THE
TWO LOCATORS

FIG 3·16

22

LOCATORS

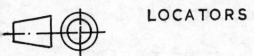

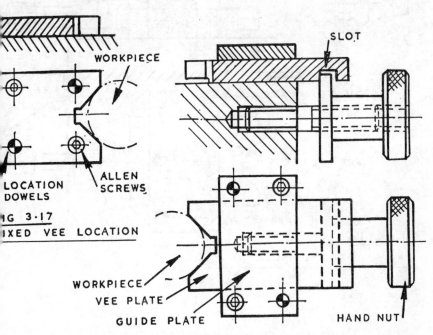

WORKPIECE

SLOT

LOCATION DOWELS

ALLEN SCREWS

FIG 3·17
FIXED VEE LOCATION

WORKPIECE

VEE PLATE

GUIDE PLATE

HAND NUT

FIG 3·18
SLIDING VEE LOCATION

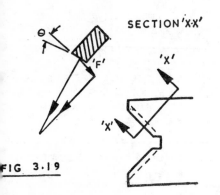

SECTION 'X-X'

FIG 3·19

WHEN VEE LOCATION IS ADJUSTABLE, THE VEE SIDES CAN BE INCLINED BY A SMALL ANGLE 'θ' TO PRODUCE A SMALL DOWNWARD CLAMPING FORCE 'F'

23

LOCATORS

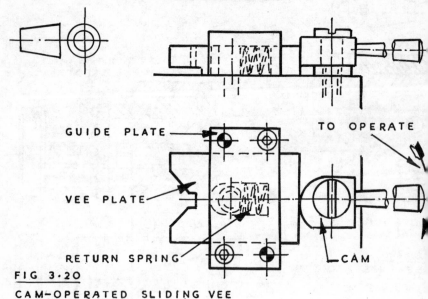

GUIDE PLATE

TO OPERATE

VEE PLATE

RETURN SPRING

CAM

FIG 3·20
CAM-OPERATED SLIDING VEE

HOLE 'A'

WORKPIECE

FIG 3·21 (a)

HOLE 'A'

WORKPIECE

FIG 3·21 (b)

CENTRE OF WORKPIECE IS
ALWAYS ON 'Y-Y' AXIS, BUT
ITS POSITION ALONG 'Y-Y'
DEPENDS UPON ITS
DIAMETER.
SUITABLE LOCATION
WHEN DRILLING HOLE 'A'

CENTRE OF WORKPIECE
ALWAYS ON 'X-X' AXIS, BUT
ITS POSITION ALONG 'Y-Y'
DEPENDS UPON ITS
DIAMETER.
UNSUITABLE LOCATION
WHEN DRILLING HOLE 'A'

APPLICATION OF VEE LOCATION

CHAPTER 4

CLAMPING AND CLAMPING DEVICES

4.10. Requirements of the clamping system

The clamping system must hold the workpiece against the cutting forces without causing damage to it.

4.20. Position of the clamps

Clamping must be at thick sections of the workpiece to avoid distortion due to clamping forces; suitable support must be introduced if the workpiece is too thin to resist deformation by the clamping forces. The clamps must be positioned so that they can be operated easily and safely by the operator, and where they can most effectively prevent movement of the workpiece.

4.30. Design of clamps

The clamp and clamping screw must be strong enough not to become distorted under the clamping force; a distorted clamp will cause insecure clamping. The clamping system must produce the required force; this depends upon the operation to be performed. For example, when clamping for turning and milling, hexagonal nuts are usually used to secure the clamp, but hand nuts are usually sufficient when drilling and reaming; this is partly due to the extent of the cutting forces involved, and partly due to the direction and nature of these forces. Hand nuts are more convenient for the operator than hexagonal nuts because a spanner is not used to tighten them; the force that the operator is able to apply can often be controlled by the size of the nut and so prevent damage to the workpiece due to excessive clamping pressure.

Clamping devices

4.40. The clamping devices illustrated represent the most common types; most of them are suitable for either hexagonal nut or hand nut clamping.

PAGE 27. SIMPLE PLATE CLAMPS

4.41. Fig. 4.1 illustrates a solid clamp; it will be seen that the toe and heel are shaped to ensure adequate clamping over a range of workpiece heights; the clamp is prevented from rotating during

B

clamping by the pin at the heel-end. The clamp stud is usually at least 10 mm diameter and must be nearer to the toe-end than the heel-end of the clamp; the clamp is released from the workpiece and supported there by the compression spring under the clamp, and the spring prevented from entering the hole in the clamp by a washer. This clamp is rotated about the stud to release the workpiece.

The clamp shown in fig. 4.2 is similar to that shown in fig. 4.1 but the clamp plate is flat because a heel pin is introduced; this pin engages in the clamp plate to prevent it rotating during clamping. Fig. 4.3 illustrates a slightly more elaborate system in which a slotted clamp plate is used so that the workpiece can be released without clamp rotation. An adjustable heel pin is often used at early machining operations where the workpiece height is likely to vary more considerably (see fig. 4.4). When a fixed heel pin is used, variation of workpiece height may cause insecure clamping by the nut; this can be offset by using a pair of spherical washers, as shown in fig. 4.5; spherical washers are sold by manufacturers of standard jig and fixture parts. The two-point clamp (fig. 4.6) is a variation of the clamps already shown and is used to clamp two workpieces or to clamp a single workpiece that is awkward to clamp using a simpler clamp.

4.42. Fig. 4.7 shows a three-point clamp of the type used to clamp a workpiece at three points; large three-point clamps are fabricated by welding from a turned cylindrical boss and lengths of T-section for the arms. Edge clamps are used when the only horizontal surface is the one to be machined; the type shown is used to clamp the workpiece on to the horizontal surface of the base, and against a suitable vertical face (see fig. 4.8). Fig. 4.9 shows a latch-type clamp; this type is very easy to operate, and the latch and stud movements are controlled (the latch is in the fully open position when the faces indicated by 'X' are in contract); the illustration shows a hand nut used to clamp the workpiece. A simple plate clamp can be used to clamp no more than two workpieces at once; if any more are presented for clamping by extending the plate, only the two larger ones will be clamped, and the others will be insecure.

4.43. The two-way clamp shown in fig. 4.11 is an extension of the latch-type clamp shown on page 28. Figs. 4.12 show a selection of button clamps; these may be fixed at one point, or removable as required.

4.44. Fig. 4.13 shows a floating pad which is often used in conjunction with the button clamp system; this prevents damage to the workpiece by allowing the screw to rotate at the point of clamping without scoring the workpiece. Cast hand-nuts of the type shown in fig. 4.14 can be purchased from the manufacturers of standard parts,

CLAMPING DEVICES

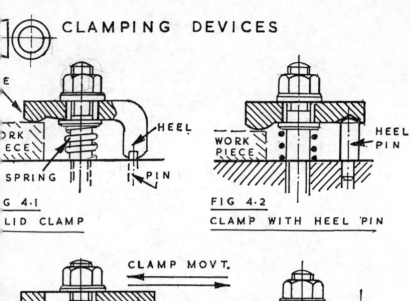

E

WORK PIECE

HEEL

SPRING | PIN

FIG 4·1
SOLID CLAMP

WORK PIECE

HEEL PIN

FIG 4·2
CLAMP WITH HEEL PIN

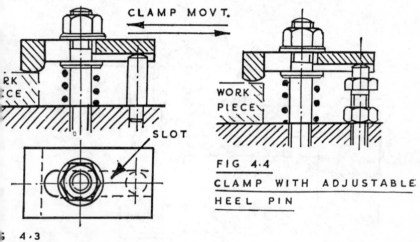

CLAMP MOVT.

WORK PIECE

SLOT

FIG 4·3
SLIDING CLAMP WITH HEEL PIN

WORK PIECE

FIG 4·4
CLAMP WITH ADJUSTABLE
HEEL PIN

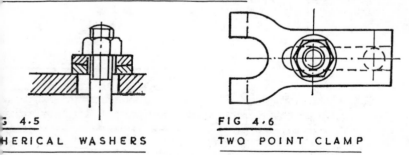

FIG 4·5
SPHERICAL WASHERS

FIG 4·6
TWO POINT CLAMP

27

CLAMPING DEVICES

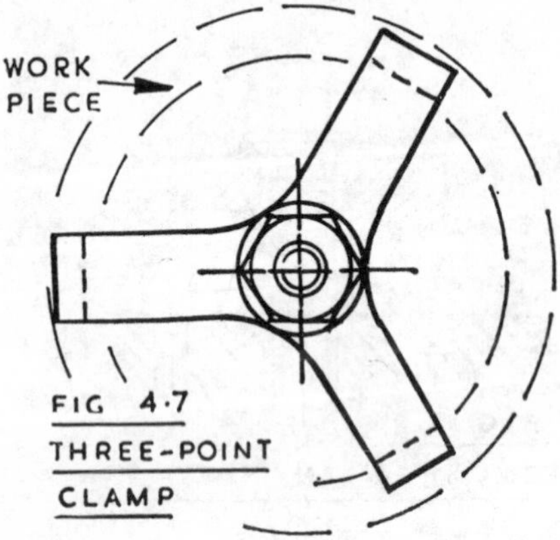

WORK PIECE

FIG 4.7
THREE-POINT
CLAMP

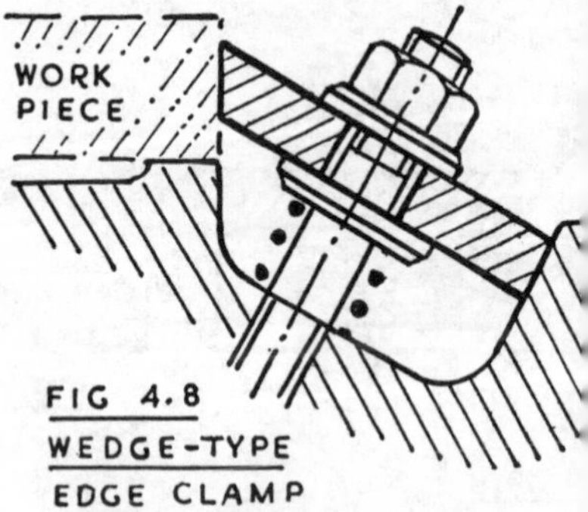

WORK PIECE

FIG 4.8
WEDGE-TYPE
EDGE CLAMP

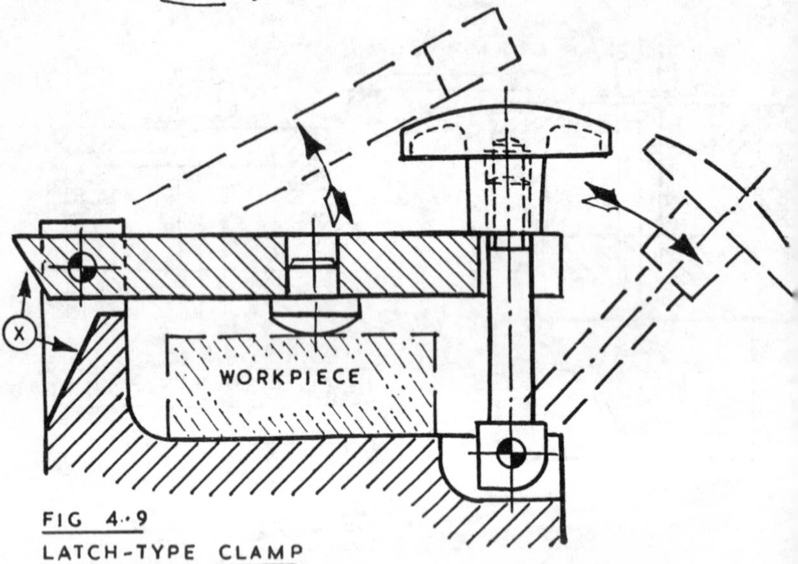

X

WORKPIECE

FIG 4.9
LATCH-TYPE CLAMP

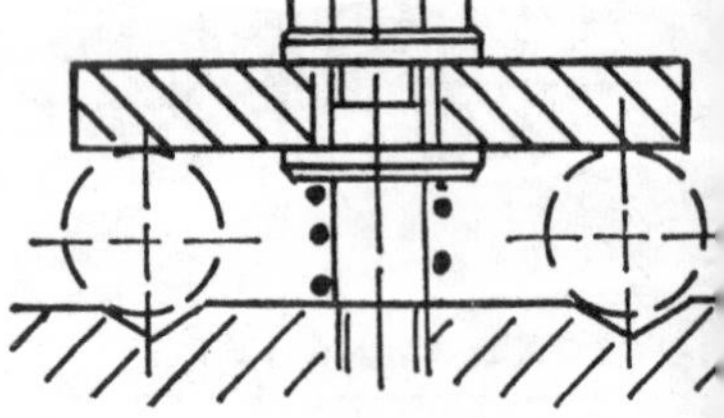

FIG 4.10
CLAMPING TWO
WORKPIECES

CLAMPING DEVICES

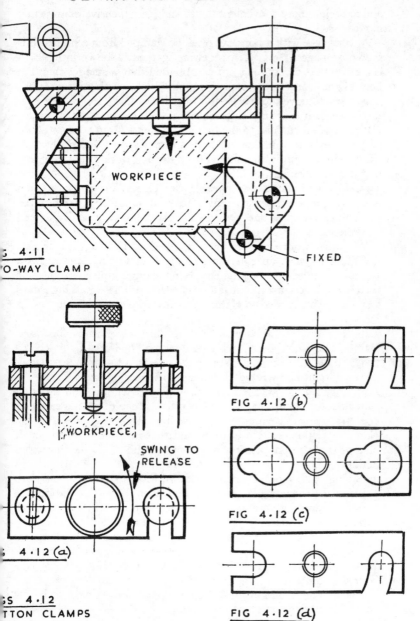

S 4·11
O-WAY CLAMP

WORKPIECE

FIXED

WORKPIECE

SWING TO
RELEASE

FIG 4·12 (b)

FIG 4·12 (c)

S 4·12 (a)

S 4·12
TTON CLAMPS

FIG 4·12 (d)

29

and are often more convenient to use and less expensive than turned hand-nuts.

A workpiece with a bore can often be clamped from a post (this is shown on page 41, fig. 5.13); a swing washer as shown in fig. 4.15 is used so that a clamping nut can be used that is smaller than the bore of the workpiece; when this method is used the nut does not have to be removed to release the workpiece. The 'Cee' washer (fig. 4.16) is used if there is insufficient room to use a swing washer; this washer is often chained to the base to prevent it from being mislaid, and if used with a horizontal post it is recessed to accept the nut, which will prevent it from falling from the post during clamping (see fig. 5.14 on page 42).

4.45. Fig. 4.17 shows a removable clamping plate in conjunction with swinging bolts; this system is less convenient than many of the preceding examples but is useful for clamping awkwardly shaped workpieces.

When two workpieces are to be clamped, and where their heights are likely to vary, an equalising clamp is useful; fig. 4.18 shows a typical arrangement, but the equalising clamping piece can also be used in conjunction with the latch-type clamp. The equalising clamp system can be applied to clamp several workpieces as illustrated in fig. 4.19.

4.46. The two examples on this page illustrate eccentric-operated clamps. Fig. 4.20 shows a swinging hook-bolt operated by an eccentric, and fig. 4.21 shows a clamp plate operated by a similar system. These systems allow rapid clamping of the workpiece.

4.47. Fig. 4.22 shows a simple cam-operated clamp, and fig. 4.23 shows a latch clamp that is cam-operated. When designing cam and eccentric-operated clamps care must be taken to ensure that the clamping action is a natural one and that in the case of the latch clamp, the clamping action is a continuation of the latch closing action.

4.48. Fig. 4.24 shows the toggle clamp; in this system a small fork movement produces a large clamp movement but when the linkage is in the clamping position a large movement at right angles to the direction of the clamping force is necessary to unlock the clamp.

Fig. 4.25 shows a quick-action hand nut which is used where it is necessary to remove the nut to release the workpiece. This nut is positioned on the stud by tipping it so that the plain portion passes over the stud; when in position it is tipped so that the threads are engaged. The hand nut illustrated is typical of the type sold by the manufacturers of standard jig parts.

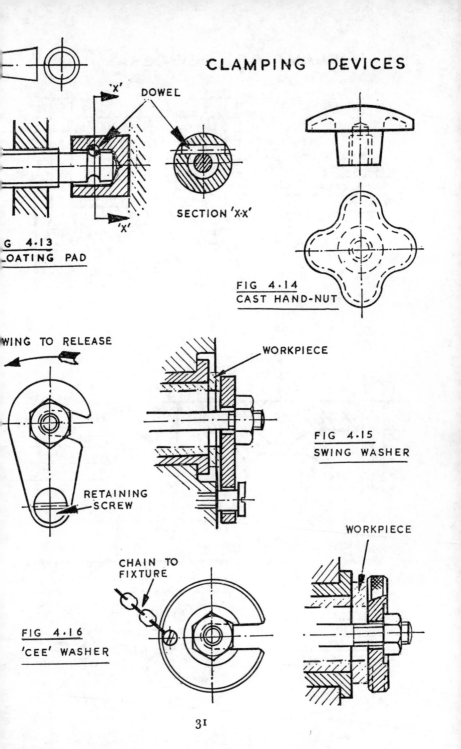

CLAMPING DEVICES

DOWEL

SECTION 'X·X'

G 4·13
LOATING PAD

FIG 4·14
CAST HAND-NUT

SWING TO RELEASE

RETAINING
SCREW

WORKPIECE

FIG 4·15
SWING WASHER

CHAIN TO
FIXTURE

WORKPIECE

FIG 4·16
'CEE' WASHER

CLAMPING DEVICES

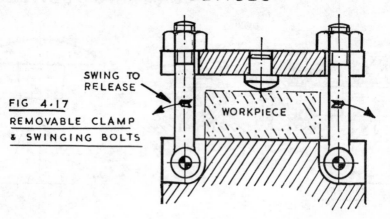

FIG 4·17
REMOVABLE CLAMP
& SWINGING BOLTS

SWING TO
RELEASE

WORKPIECE

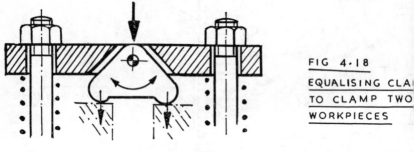

FIG 4·18
EQUALISING CLA
TO CLAMP TWO
WORKPIECES

FIG 4·19
EQUALISING CLAMP
SYSTEM TO CLAMP
FOUR WORKPIECES

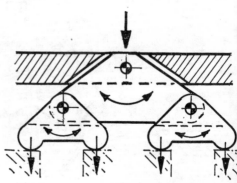

CLAMPING DEVICES

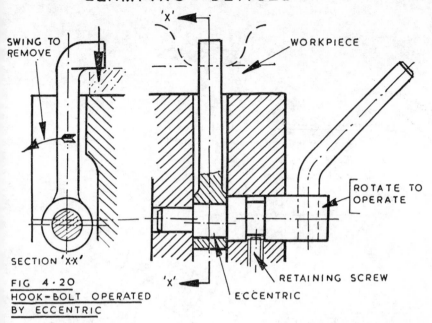

SWING TO REMOVE

WORKPIECE

'x'

ROTATE TO OPERATE

SECTION 'X-X'

FIG 4·20
HOOK-BOLT OPERATED
BY ECCENTRIC

'x'

RETAINING SCREW

ECCENTRIC

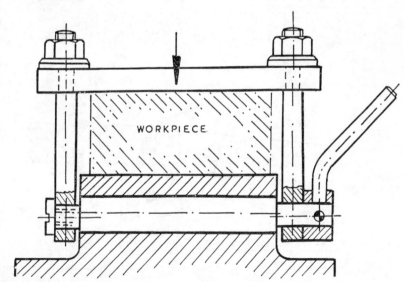

WORKPIECE.

FIG 4·21
ECCENTRIC-OPERATED CLAMPING SYSTEM

CLAMPING DEVICES

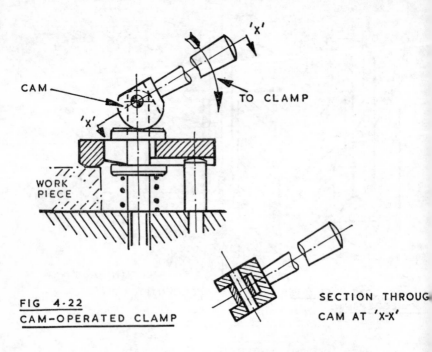

CAM

'x'

TO CLAMP

'x'

WORK
PIECE

FIG 4·22
CAM—OPERATED CLAMP

SECTION THROUG
CAM AT 'X-X'

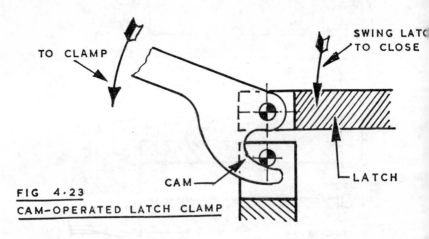

TO CLAMP

SWING LATC
TO CLOSE

CAM

LATCH

FIG 4·23
CAM—OPERATED LATCH CLAMP

CLAMPING DEVICES

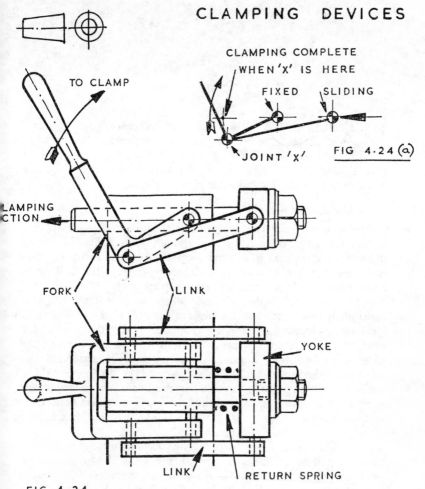

CLAMPING COMPLETE
WHEN 'X' IS HERE

FIXED   SLIDING

JOINT 'X'   FIG 4·24 (a)

TO CLAMP

CLAMPING
ACTION

FORK   LINK

YOKE

LINK   RETURN SPRING

FIG 4·24
TOGGLE CLAMP

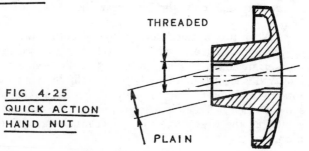

THREADED

FIG 4·25
QUICK ACTION
HAND NUT

PLAIN

35

CHAPTER 5

DRILL JIGS

5.10. Drill jigs are used to hold the workpiece when drilling, reaming, counterboring, countersinking, spotfacing and tapping.

With the exception of taps, the tools are usually guided during cutting, and so drill jigs must incorporate means of guiding the tools, in addition to location and clamping systems.

5.20. Guiding the tools

The tools are guided by means of holes in the drill plate which is located relative to the workpiece. Although the tools may be guided directly by the plate, it is usual to guide them in direct, or case-hardened steel bushes that are an interference fit in the drill plate. Some typical drill bushes are shown on page 37.

5.21. Headed drill bushes are used when the hole depth must be controlled; good seating of the bush in the hole in the drill plate is ensured by chamfering the hole, and undercutting the head of the bush. A generous lead is provided, and in order to prevent the swarf from becoming jammed between the drill plate and the workpiece, the bush is either placed close to the workpiece so that the swarf can only escape through the bush, or is placed far enough away from the workpiece to permit the swarf to escape between it and the workpiece (see figs. 5.1). Headless drill bushes are used where the hole depth is not important.

5.22. Special bushes are used for awkward workpieces; fig. 5.3 shows a drill bush that is shaped to prevent drill run due to the sloping workpiece face, and fig. 5.4 shows an extended drill bush as used when a hole is to be drilled in a face that is some distance from the drill plate. When the drill bush is particularly long, its bore is relieved so that only the end near the workpiece controls the tool.

5.23. When two or more tools are to cut on the same axis, as when drilling and then reaming a hole, slip bushes are used. A typical slip bush arrangement is shown in fig. 5.5; a slip bush is used for each tool, and is located in a liner bush. The slip bush is prevented from rotating and running up the cutting tool by a retaining screw as shown; when a large-diameter cutting tool is also used (as when spotfacing the workpiece) the tool is usually guided by the liner bush.

DRILL BUSHES

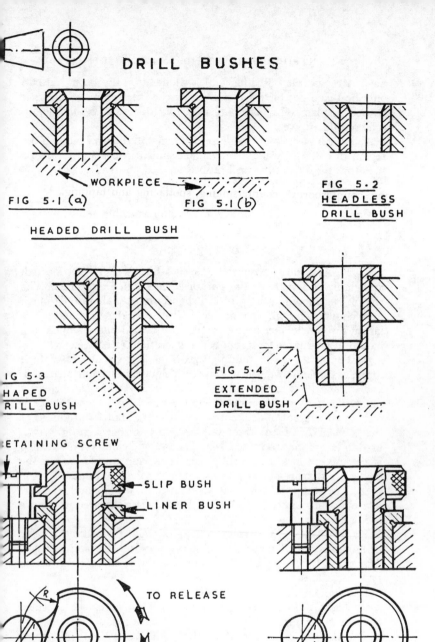

FIG 5·1 (a)

FIG 5·1 (b)

WORKPIECE

HEADED DRILL BUSH

FIG 5·2
HEADLESS
DRILL BUSH

FIG 5·3
SHAPED
DRILL BUSH

FIG 5·4
EXTENDED
DRILL BUSH

RETAINING SCREW

SLIP BUSH

LINER BUSH

TO RELEASE

DRILL ROTATION

FIG 5·5
SLIP BUSH ARRANGEMENT

FIG 5·6
RENEWABLE BUSH
ARRANGEMENT

37

5.24. A renewable bush (fig. 5.6) is similar to a slip bush, but can only be taken out of the liner by removing the retaining screw; it is used in place of an ordinary drill bush if it is to be frequently renewed due to wear.

5.25. A drill bush can be used to lightly clamp the workpiece in the region of cutting by the arrangement shown in fig. 5.7; it will be seen that the axis of the drill bush is located positively.

5.26. Hole depth can be controlled by holding the tool in a special socket incorporating a stop nut which is set by means of a special setting gauge; fig. 5.8 illustrates a drill stop assembly and its setting.

Drill jig types

5.30. Fig. 5.9 shows a typical plate jig which is sighted or located, and clamped directly on the workpiece and bolted in position. The channel jig shown in fig. 5.10 is a slightly more elaborate jig made from channel section. The local jig is a plate jig that is bolted to the facing to be machined; the workpiece is located and clamped to a base that is suitable for a number of operations (see fig. 5.11).

5.31. Fig. 5.12 shows a solid jig that is made from a block of steel; in the example shown, the workpiece is clamped by a button clamp, and burr grooves are provided so that the workpiece can be easily removed. (Two grooves are required because one burr will be produced at the point of drill entry, and a second burr is produced at the point of drill break-through.) The post jig shown in fig. 5.13 is used to locate the workpiece from its bore by means of a post which is also used to locate the drill plate. The swing washer enables the drill plate to be removed without removing the hand nut.

5.32. The post jig shown in fig. 5.14 is used for drilling and reaming; a 'cee' washer is used in this example to obviate the need to remove the hand nut.

Fig. 5.15 shows an angular post jig of welded construction. The drill bush is extended and shaped to prevent drill run, and yet allow removal of the workpiece. The clamping nut is of the quick action type because the smallness of the workpiece bore demands that the nut be removed when the workpiece is removed.

5.33. Fig. 5.16 illustrates a pot jig in which the workpiece is located from its outside in a bush, and the drill bush is located on a post; the workpiece is supported at the point of drilling, and swarf clearances are provided; the drill plate is located to line up with the swarf clearance grooves.

The pot jig shown in fig. 5.17 is a similar type, but the workpiece is only placed in the pot to support the flange, and the drill plate is located directly in the workpiece bore.

DRILL BUSHES AND DEPTH CONTROL

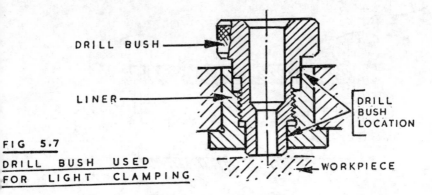

DRILL BUSH

LINER

DRILL BUSH LOCATION

WORKPIECE

FIG 5.7
DRILL BUSH USED
FOR LIGHT CLAMPING.

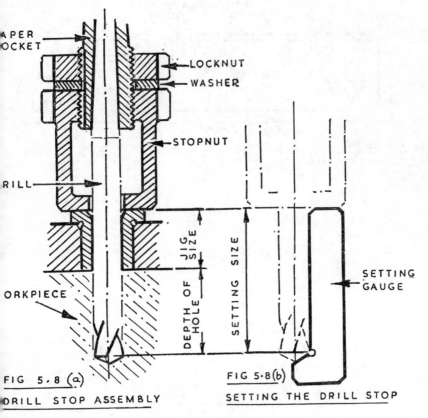

TAPER SOCKET

LOCKNUT

WASHER

STOPNUT

DRILL

JIG SIZE

DEPTH OF HOLE

SETTING SIZE

SETTING GAUGE

WORKPIECE

FIG 5.8 (a)
DRILL STOP ASSEMBLY

FIG 5.8 (b)
SETTING THE DRILL STOP

DEPTH CONTROL

DRILL JIG TYPES

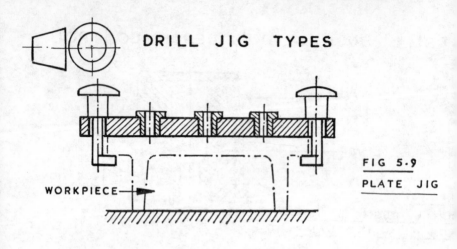

FIG 5.9
PLATE JIG

WORKPIECE

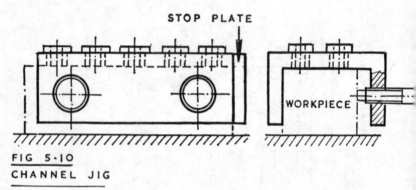

STOP PLATE

WORKPIECE

FIG 5·10
CHANNEL JIG

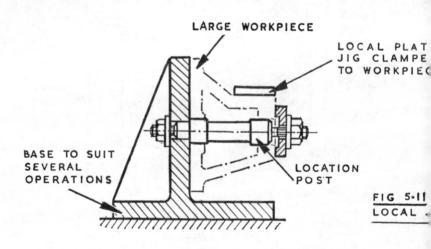

LARGE WORKPIECE

LOCAL PLAT
JIG CLAMPE
TO WORKPIEC

BASE TO SUIT
SEVERAL
OPERATIONS

LOCATION
POST

FIG 5·11
LOCAL

40

DRILL JIG TYPES

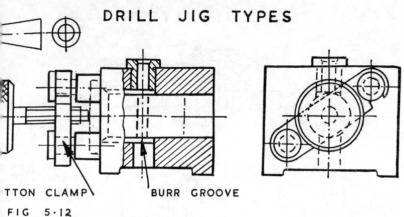

TTON CLAMP   BURR GROOVE

FIG 5·12
SOLID JIG

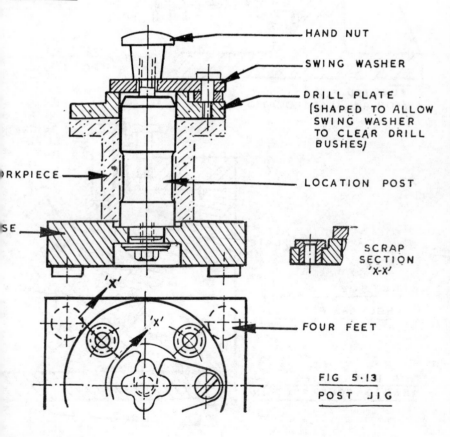

HAND NUT

SWING WASHER

DRILL PLATE
(SHAPED TO ALLOW
SWING WASHER
TO CLEAR DRILL
BUSHES)

ORKPIECE

LOCATION POST

SE

SCRAP
SECTION
'X-X'

FOUR FEET

FIG 5·13
POST JIG

41

DRILL JIG TYPES

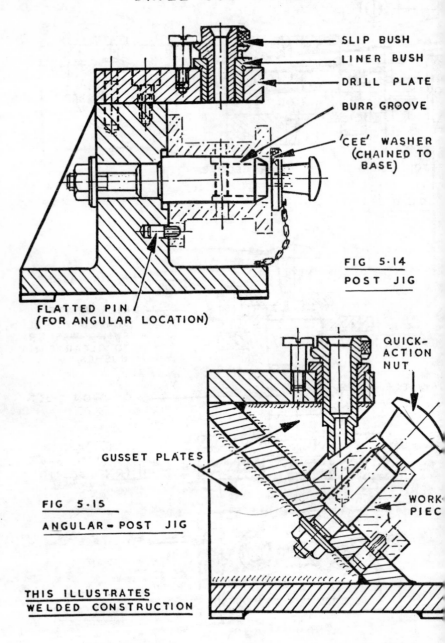

SLIP BUSH

LINER BUSH

DRILL PLATE

BURR GROOVE

'CEE' WASHER
(CHAINED TO
BASE)

FIG 5·14
POST JIG

FLATTED PIN
(FOR ANGULAR LOCATION)

QUICK-
ACTION
NUT

GUSSET PLATES

FIG 5·15
ANGULAR - POST JIG

WORK
PIECE

THIS ILLUSTRATES
WELDED CONSTRUCTION

42

DRILL JIG TYPES

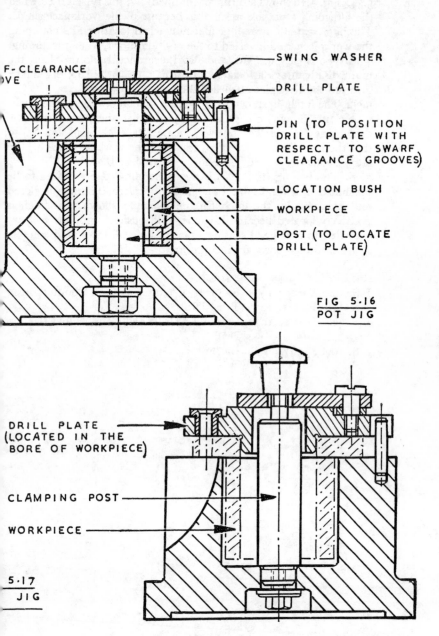

F- CLEARANCE
OVE

SWING WASHER

DRILL PLATE

PIN (TO POSITION
DRILL PLATE WITH
RESPECT TO SWARF
CLEARANCE GROOVES)

LOCATION BUSH

WORKPIECE

POST (TO LOCATE
DRILL PLATE)

FIG 5.16
POT JIG

DRILL PLATE
(LOCATED IN THE
BORE OF WORKPIECE)

CLAMPING POST

WORKPIECE

5.17
JIG

5.34. Fig. 5.18 shows a turnover (or open) jig; this type is used when the foregoing types are unsuitable because of the workpiece shape. The jig is seated on the four foot-nuts when locating and clamping the workpiece, and inverted to the position shown when machining. This type is easy to load, and swarf clearance is no problem; the main disadvantage associated with this type is the lack of support given to the workpiece beneath the point of cutting.

5.35. The latch jig shown in fig. 5.19 is an elaboration of the latch-type clamp shown on page 28 (fig. 4.9). When the latch carries the drill bushes, it must be positively located (faces 'X' and slot 'Y') so that the bush bores are vertical whatever the workpiece height; the latch is clamped by nut 'A' and the workpiece by screw 'B'.

5.36. The box jig (fig. 5.20) is used when holes are required to be machined in several faces in a small workpiece. The box is closed and clamped by the latch (in the example shown, this latch is positively located because it carries drill bushes). Suitable feet are provided to give good seating when drilling all faces, and suitable swarf clearance ports are incorporated.

REFERENCES

B.S. 122: Part 2: 1964. Reamers, Countersinks and Counterbores.
B.S. 328: Part 1: 1959. Twist Drills.
B.S. 328: Part 2: 1972. Combined Drills and Countersinks (Centre Drills).
B.S. 1098: 1967.   Jig Bushes.

DRILL JIG TYPES

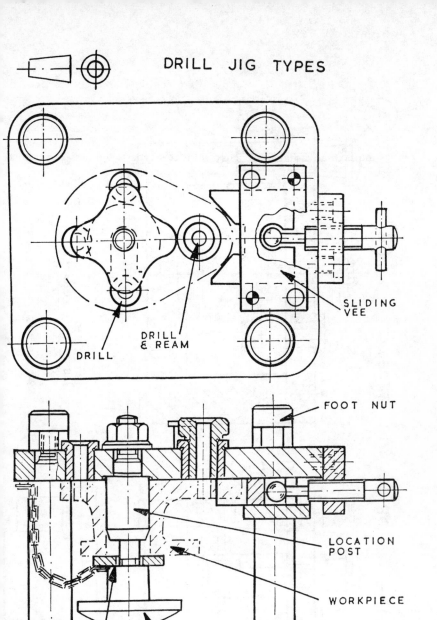

SLIDING VEE

DRILL & REAM

DRILL

FOOT NUT

LOCATION POST

WORKPIECE

'CEE' WASHER (CHAINED TO BASE)

QUICK-ACTION NUT

FIG 5·18

TURNOVER JIG

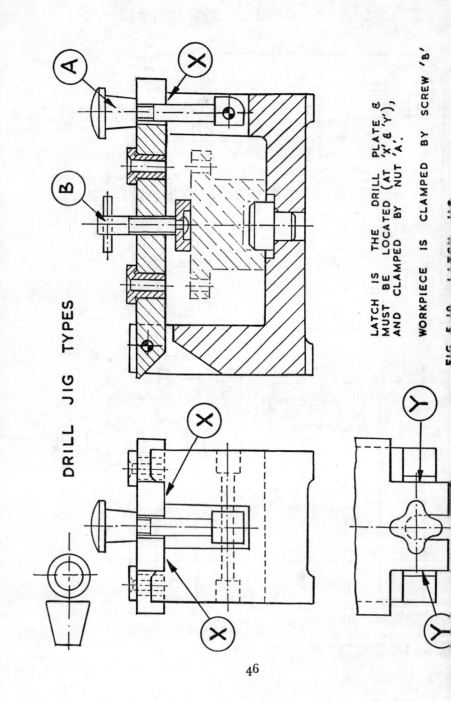

DRILL JIG TYPES

LATCH IS THE DRILL PLATE & MUST BE LOCATED (AT 'X' & 'Y'), AND CLAMPED BY NUT 'A'.

WORKPIECE IS CLAMPED BY SCREW 'B'

FIG 5.10 LATCH JIG

46

DRILL JIG TYPES

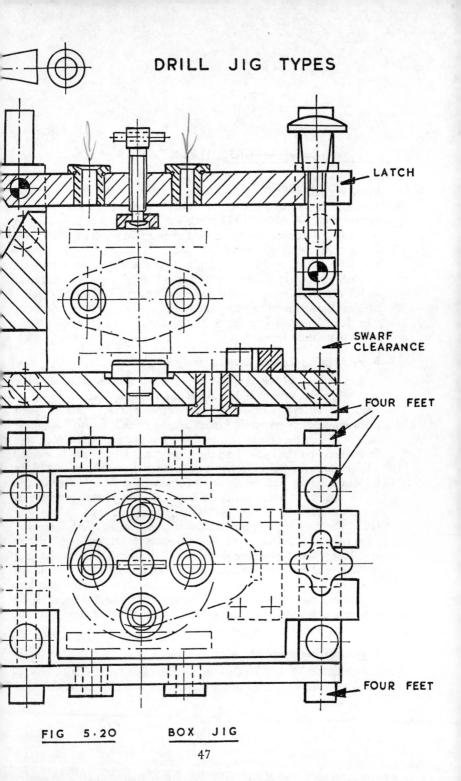

LATCH

SWARF CLEARANCE

FOUR FEET

FOUR FEET

FIG 5.20   BOX JIG

47

CHAPTER 6

MILLING FIXTURES

6.10. A milling fixture is located accurately on the machine table and then bolted in position; the table is positioned relative to the cutter or cutters with the aid of the setting block. The workpiece is located on the fixture base and then clamped in position. The cutter is not guided during cutting.

6.11. The location and clamping systems are similar to those used for drill jigs, but as the cutting forces are high, interrupted, and tend to lift the workpiece, the clamping forces must be big; hexagonal nuts are usually used to clamp the workpiece rather than hand nuts. The details that are peculiar to milling fixtures are the setting block and the location tenons.

6.20. Milling fixture details (see page 49)

The **setting block** as shown in fig. 6.1 is located relative to the fixture location system and retained in position by screws; it has two hardened setting faces, so that the table can be positioned both horizontally and vertically (note that the table is located from one side of the cutter only). The table setting is done with a 0.25 mm feeler between the cutter and the setting face so that the block will not be damaged by the cutter during machining. The setting block is positioned so that the cutter is between the vertical face of the block and the operator during setting; this arrangement gives maximum convenience for the operator during setting.

6.21. The two **tenons** (one tenon is shown in fig. 6.2) are made from casehardened steel and are located on the underside of the fixture base; these two tenons sit in ONE of the tee slots that run along the length of the machine table so that the fixture is located relative to the table feed; the two tenons should be as far apart as possible, to produce maximum accuracy. The fixture is bolted to the table by two or four tee bolts that are placed in the tee slots (these bolts are not called up as part of the fixture).

6.30. Milling methods

The fixture design depends upon the milling methods to be employed; some variations of simple milling are illustrated on pages 51–53.

MILLING FIXTURE DETAILS

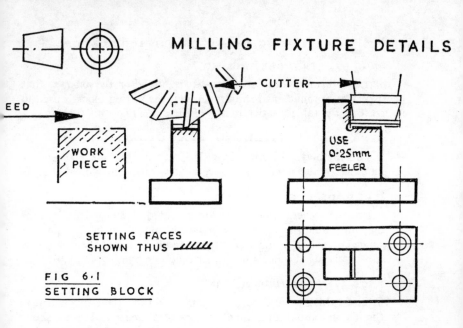

EED →

CUTTER →

WORK PIECE

USE 0·25mm FEELER

SETTING FACES SHOWN THUS ⁄⁄⁄⁄⁄

FIG 6·1
SETTING BLOCK

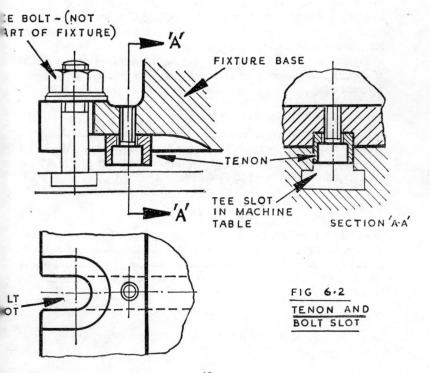

E BOLT - (NOT ⁀RT OF FIXTURE)

FIXTURE BASE

TENON

TEE SLOT IN MACHINE TABLE

SECTION 'A-A'

LT ⁀OT

FIG 6·2
TENON AND BOLT SLOT

PAGE 51. STRADDLE MILLING

6.31. In this method two cutters are mounted on the arbor so that two faces are machined simultaneously; the setting block is used to position the table relative to one of the cutters (see fig. 6.3).

GANG MILLING

This method is illustrated by fig. 6.4; three or more cutters are mounted on the arbor so that several faces can be machined at once.

STRING OR LINE MILLING

In which several workpieces are mounted along the length of the machine table so that they can be machined during one pass. A single cutter or a number of cutters can be used, and the workpieces can be arranged in a single line or a double line (see fig. 6.6).

PAGE 52. PENDULUM MILLING

6.32. In this system cutting takes place during table movement to the left and also during table movement to the right. Fig. 6.7 shows an example in which two slots are required at right-angles. The workpiece is held in an indexing fixture (see Chapter 8) and it can be rotated about its axis at the end of the first pass so that the second slot can be produced during the return pass.

Fig. 6.8 shows an arrangement in which two workpieces are held in an indexing fixture, so that at the end of the first pass they can be interchanged and cutting continued during the return pass.

PAGE 53. PROFILE MILLING

6.33. Complicated profiles can be milled by holding the workpiece in a fixture that incorporates a profile plate, and holding the cutter in a special holder with a roller follower, and the profile on the profile plate be followed by hand feed.

Special vice jaws

6.40. The machine vice is the simplest piece of milling machine equipment; it can be adapted to accommodate awkwardly shaped workpieces, or to incorporate a location system. The illustrations on page 54 show some typical special vice jaws as used to adapt standard vices.

MILLING METHODS

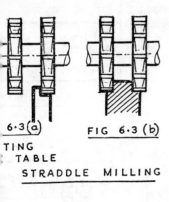

6·3(a)

TING
TABLE

FIG 6·3 (b)

STRADDLE MILLING

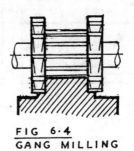

FIG 6·4
GANG MILLING

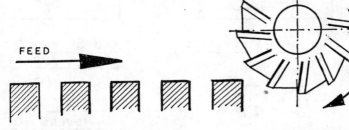

FEED

FIG 6·5
STRING MILLING

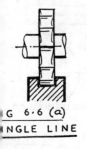

G 6·6 (a)
NGLE LINE

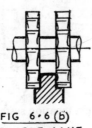

FIG 6·6 (b)
SINGLE LINE
STRADDLE
MILLING

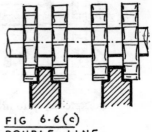

FIG 6·6 (c)
DOUBLE LINE
GANG MILLING

STRING MILLING METHODS

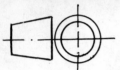

PENDULUM MILLING

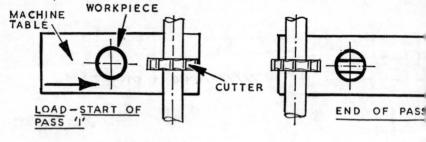

LOAD—START OF
PASS '1'

END OF PASS

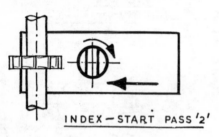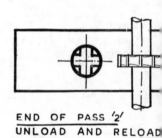

INDEX—START PASS '2'

END OF PASS '2'
UNLOAD AND RELOAD

WORKPIECE

FIG 6·7

PENDULUM MILLING
(SINGLE CUTTER—O
WORKPIECE CUT AT
TIME)

CUTTER GANG

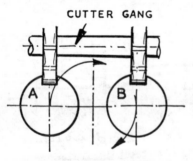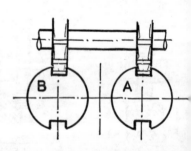

PASS '1' — THEN INDEX
AS SHOWN

PASS '2'   THEN UNLOA
AND RELOAD

FIG 6·8 PENDULUM MILLING (TWO
WORKPIECES CUT AT A TIME
WITH CUTTER GANG)

PROFILE MILLING

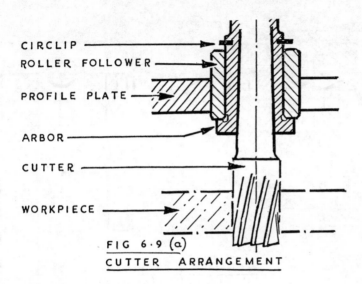

CIRCLIP
ROLLER FOLLOWER
PROFILE PLATE
ARBOR
CUTTER
WORKPIECE

FIG 6·9 (a)
CUTTER ARRANGEMENT

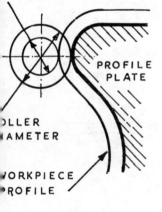

CUTTER DIAMETER

PROFILE PLATE

ROLLER DIAMETER

WORKPIECE PROFILE

FIG 6·9 (b)
OUTSIDE PROFILE

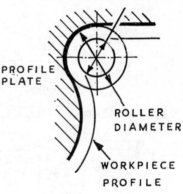

CUTTER DIAMETER

PROFILE PLATE

ROLLER DIAMETER

WORKPIECE PROFILE

FIG 6·9 (c)
INSIDE PROFILE

CUTTER, ROLLER. WORKPIECE. & PROFILE
PLATE RELATIONSHIP

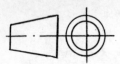

SPECIAL VICE JAWS

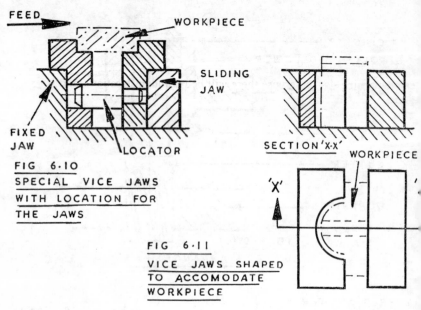

FEED

WORKPIECE

SLIDING JAW

FIXED JAW

LOCATOR

FIG 6·10
SPECIAL VICE JAWS
WITH LOCATION FOR
THE JAWS

SECTION 'X-X'

WORKPIECE

'X'

FIG 6·11
VICE JAWS SHAPED
TO ACCOMODATE
WORKPIECE

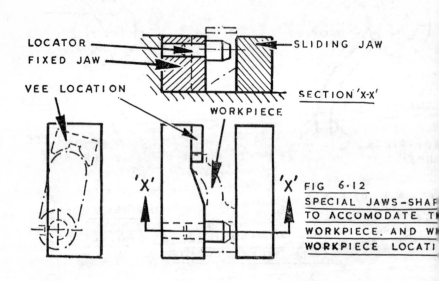

LOCATOR

FIXED JAW

VEE LOCATION

SLIDING JAW

SECTION 'X-X'

WORKPIECE

'X'

'X'

FIG 6·12
SPECIAL JAWS-SHAF
TO ACCOMODATE T
WORKPIECE. AND W
WORKPIECE LOCATI

54

Milling fixture types

PAGE 56. SIMPLE MILLING FIXTURE

6.50. Fig. 6.13 shows the arrangement for a simple fixture. The fixture is located on the machine table by two tenons that locate in the same machine slot (otherwise there will be redundant location), and is bolted to the machine using the tee slot. The workpiece is located from two holes using a full diameter location pin and a flatted location pin (note that the locating parts of the flatted pin lie on an arc whose centre is that of the full diameter pin). The workpiece is clamped using two spanner-tightened, heavy duty clamps because of the high forces when milling. The 'cutter setting' is obtained using a setting block with two setting faces – one for 'depth' and the other for 'transverse setting'.

PAGE 57. LINE, OR STRING MILLING FIXTURE

6.51. Fig. 16.4 shows an arrangement in which five cylindrical workpieces are located in line and a slot milled in the end of each. The workpieces are located and clamped with one spanner-tightened screw. The location of the fixture, the method of securing it, and the setting system is as in the previous example.

6.62. INDEXING MILLING FIXTURES are described in Chapter 8.

REFERENCES

B.S. 122: Part I: 1953. Milling Cutters.

MILLING FIXTURE TYPES

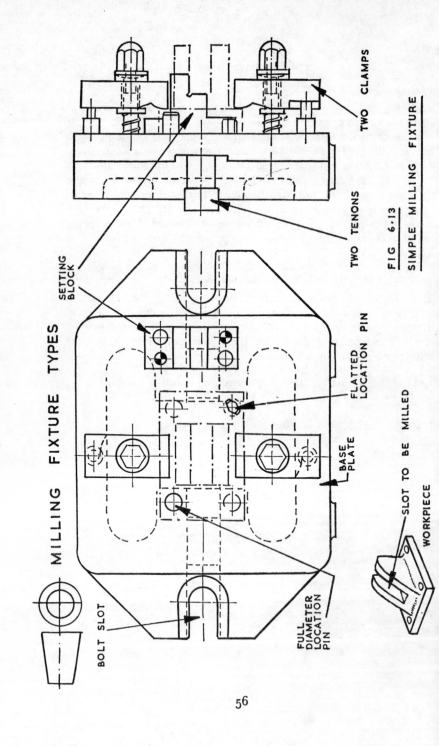

SETTING BLOCK

FLATTED LOCATION PIN

BASE PLATE

FULL DIAMETER LOCATION PIN

BOLT SLOT

TWO CLAMPS

TWO TENONS

SLOT TO BE MILLED

WORKPIECE

FIG 6·13
SIMPLE MILLING FIXTURE

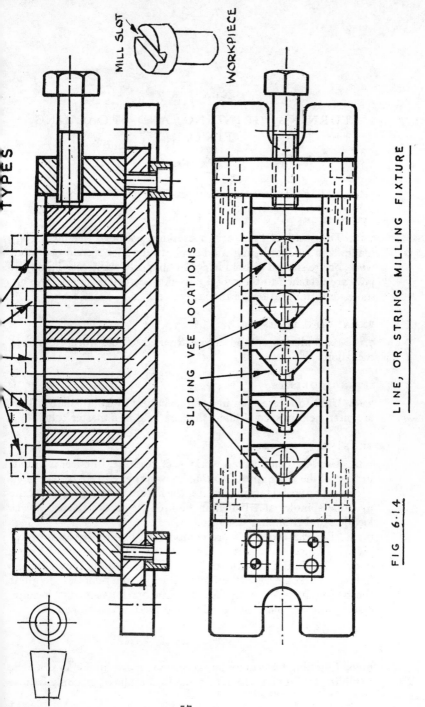

TYPES

MILL SLOT

WORKPIECE

SLIDING VEE LOCATIONS

LINE, OR STRING MILLING FIXTURE

FIG 6·14

57

CHAPTER 7

TURNING, GRINDING, AND BROACHING FIXTURES

Turning

7.10. Holding devices for turning include the following:

JAW CHUCKS

7.11. These are used for early operations. Soft jaws (see fig. 7.1(*a*)) made from casehardening mild steel are used for second-operation work, or are shaped to hold irregular-shaped workpieces. These soft jaws are attached to the radial jaw-slides by collar screws. Fig. 7.1 show some applications of the jaw chuck.

EXPANDING POSTS (fig. 7.2)

7.12. Expanding posts and arbors are used to hold workpieces from their bore.

SPRING COLLETS

7.13. Used to locate bars in capstan lathes; awkward-shaped bars are often held in special liners that are held in a master collet.

TURNING FIXTURES

7.14. Used for complicated workpieces, and are, in effect a simplification of the technique of bolting the workpiece to a faceplate. Fig. 7.3 shows a typical turning fixture; the fixture body is located on the machine spindle, and bolted in position; it carries the workpiece location and clamping systems.

7.141. Fig. 7.4 shows a more complicated fixture; here the workpiece is located and clamped to a shelf that projects from the fixture body. The fixture illustrated incorporates a balance weight (the fixture would otherwise be out of balance) and a pilot bush to guide the boring bar. A setting face, machined relative to the location system, and a typical hardened setting piece is also shown.

Grinding

7.20. Grinding fixtures for surface grinding are similar in principle to milling fixtures but are more accurate. Similarly, grinding fixtures

TURNING

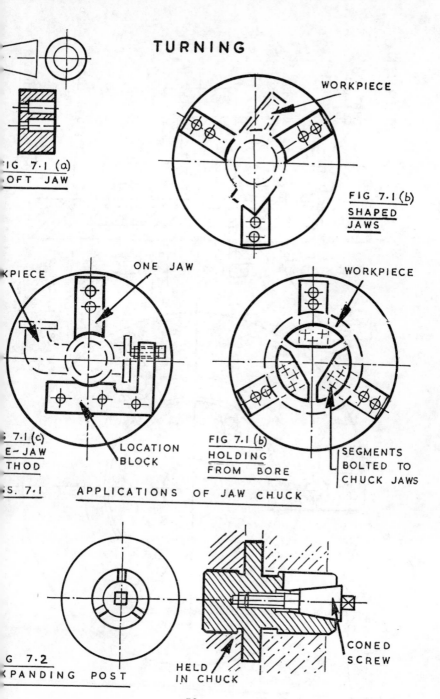

FIG 7.1 (a)
SOFT JAW

WORKPIECE

FIG 7.1 (b)
SHAPED JAWS

WORKPIECE   ONE JAW

WORKPIECE

FIG 7.1 (c)
ONE-JAW METHOD

LOCATION BLOCK

FIG 7.1 (b)
HOLDING FROM BORE

SEGMENTS BOLTED TO CHUCK JAWS

FIGS. 7.1   APPLICATIONS OF JAW CHUCK

FIG 7.2
EXPANDING POST

HELD IN CHUCK

CONED SCREW

59

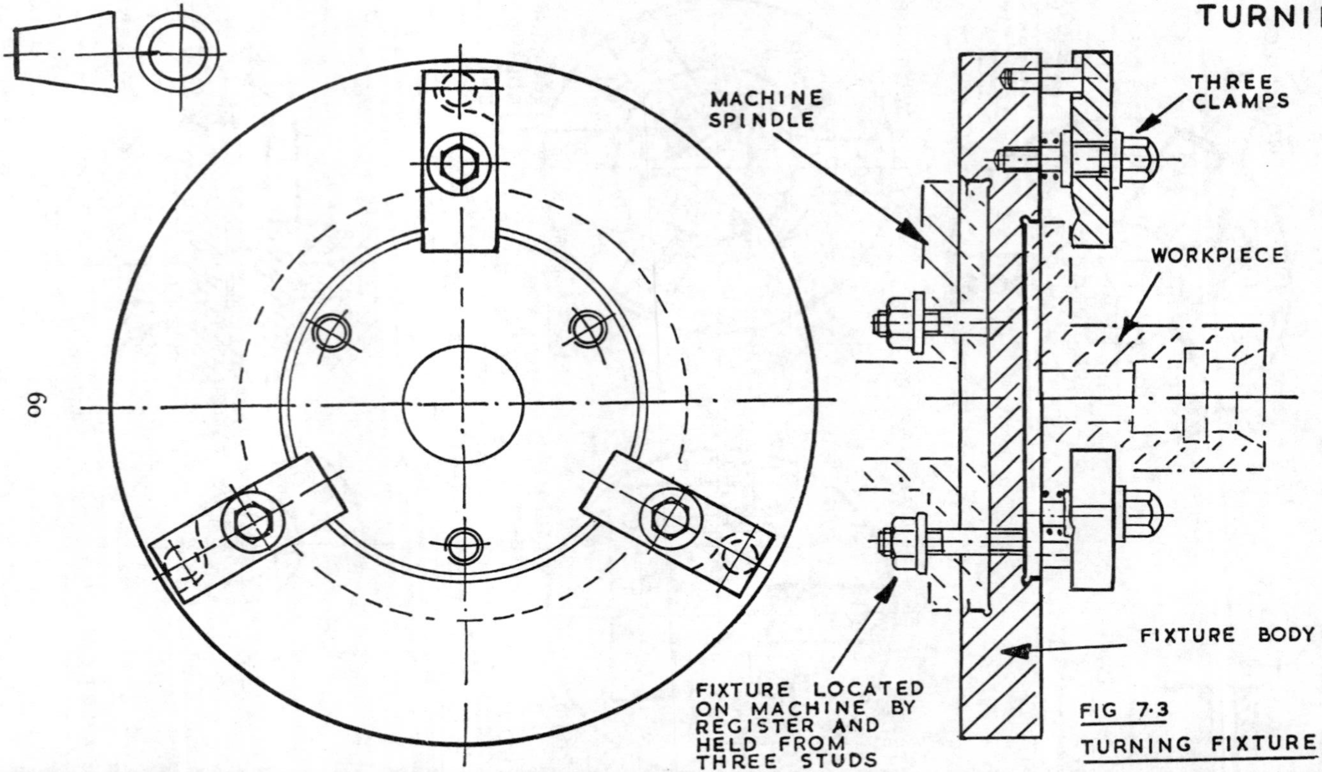

TURNING

THREE CLAMPS

WORKPIECE

FIXTURE BODY

MACHINE SPINDLE

FIXTURE LOCATED ON MACHINE BY REGISTER AND HELD FROM THREE STUDS

FIG 7.3
TURNING FIXTURE

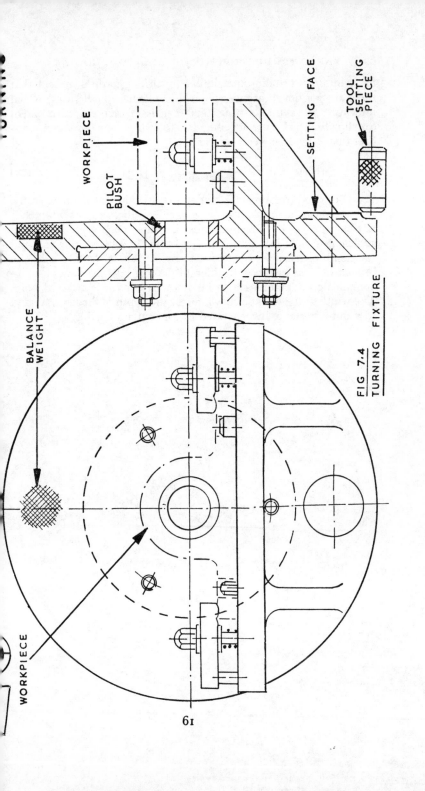

WORKPIECE

BALANCE
WEIGHT

WORKPIECE

PILOT
BUSH

SETTING FACE

TOOL
SETTING
PIECE

FIG 7.4
TURNING FIXTURE

61

for cylindrical grinding are similar to turning fixtures, except that these are positioned accurately on the machine spindle using a dial indicator; a ground setting diameter is therefore incorporated. Small cylindrical parts are often located from their bore on a mandrel that is held between centres.

Broaching

7.30. Two typical broaching adaptors are illustrated on page 63. Fig. 7.5 shows a simple keyway broaching adaptor; this adaptor is not clamped to the machine table because the broaching force is sufficient to hold it in position. The broach is located in a slot, and the depth of the keyway controlled by a packing piece so that one broach can cut keyways of different depths. Fig. 7.6 shows a more complicated adaptor used to broach a keyway in a tapered bore. The width of the workpiece will affect the depth of the keyway, and so a nut-adjuster is incorporated to compensate for this.

BROACHING

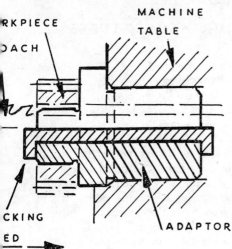

WORKPIECE

BROACH

MACHINE TABLE

ADAPTOR

BACKING

FEED

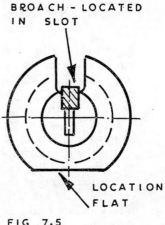

BROACH - LOCATED IN SLOT

LOCATION FLAT

FIG 7·5
KEYWAY BROACHING

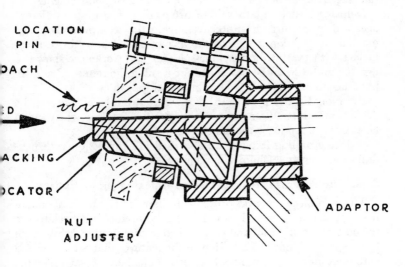

LOCATION PIN

BROACH

FEED

BACKING

LOCATOR

NUT ADJUSTER

ADAPTOR

FIG 7·6 BROACHING A KEYWAY IN A TAPERED BORE

63

CHAPTER 8

INDEXING JIGS AND FIXTURES

8.10. Indexing jigs and fixtures are used when it is necessary to move the workpiece relative to the machine table or spindle between machining various features during an operation.

8.20. Some typical applications of indexing are illustrated on page 65 (these illustrations are not to the same scale).

Fig. 8.1 shows a long strip that is to be drilled in several places along its length; if a non-indexing jig is used the machine must have a large table and its spindle must have a large 'coverage'. In the example shown the holes are in line and are equispaced; only one drill bush is required, and the workpiece is positioned under it before each hole is drilled. If the holes are not all on the same centreline, or if they are not equispaced, more than one drill bush is required; in the example shown in fig. 8.2 the holes are in groups of three, and so three drill bushes are required, and the workpiece is positioned so that three holes are drilled between each indexing movement.

Indexing is used in lathework if two or more features on different axes are to be turned without removing the workpiece from the machine to position it so that the axis of each feature in turn coincides with that of the machine-spindle. The workpiece shown in figs. 8.3 and 8.4 can be positioned for turning the stems 'A' and 'B' by either linear indexing or by rotational indexing.

Rotational indexing is also used when several holes are to be drilled on a large-diameter pitch circle (fig. 8.5), or when radial holes or slots are to be machined (fig. 8.6).

Indexing milling fixtures are also used in conjunction with pendulum milling (see Chapter 6, page 52).

8.30. The essential features of an indexing jig or fixture

The workpiece must be located and clamped to a movable member that can, in turn, be indexed to the required position relative to the cutter or drill bush, and then locked in that position whilst each feature is machined. In addition to the features that are associated with non-indexing equipment, a slide or a bearing, an indexing device, and a device to lock the movable member must be incorporated. The slide or bearing and the locking device must be designed to suit the operation to be performed, but it must be emphasised that the locking device for the movable member must be **separate** from the workpiece clamp.

APPLICATIONS OF INDEXING

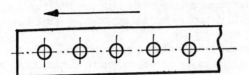

FIG 8·1
LINEAR
INDEXING

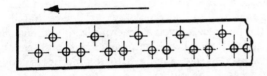

FIG 8·2
LINEAR
INDEXING

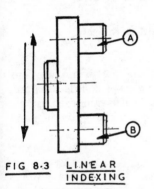

FIG 8·3   LINEAR
INDEXING

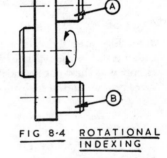

FIG 8·4   ROTATIONAL
INDEXING

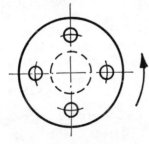

FIG 8·5   ROTATIONAL
INDEXING

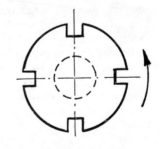

FIG 8·6 ROTATIONAL
INDEXING

8.40. Indexing devices (see page 67)

Usually the indexing member is located in the fixed part of the jig or fixture and engages in slots or holes that are suitably spaced in the moving member or indexing plate.

Fig. 8.7 shows a simple lever indexing system in which the lever engages in rectangular slots in the moving member; the lever can be spring-loaded if required.

The spring-loaded ball shown in fig. 8.8 is useful for light work, but is a less positive indexing system than the other types illustrated; the ball is retained by a plate, and the spring is guided by a pin.

The plunger system (fig. 8.9) is a commonly used device that gives positive location; the plunger is given a generous lead, and engages in bushes in the movable member. The plunger and bush can be coned, or specially shaped as shown in fig. 8.10, to prevent reduction in accuracy due to wear of the plunger end, or the index plate.

The plunger can be spring-loaded as shown in fig. 8.11, or actuated by a rack and pinion system as shown in fig. 8.12.

Typical indexing jigs and fixtures

PAGE 68

8.50. Fig. 8.13 shows a simple indexing drill jig to produce four radial holes in the workpiece shown. The workpiece is located and clamped to the rotating indexing member, which is indexed using a lever system, and locked in position during machining, by the hand nut.

PAGE 69

8.51. Fig. 8.14 shows a typical fixture used to index a heavy workpiece about a vertical axis. Before each indexing movement the moving member is raised from the top surface of the base of the fixture by operating the lever locking device, so that the moving member and workpiece is supported via the thrust bearing, and can be easily rotated during indexing; the indexing system is of the rack and pinion type. After indexing, the moving member is lowered by operating the locking device lever, so that it is locked against the top face of the base during machining.

INDEXING DEVICES

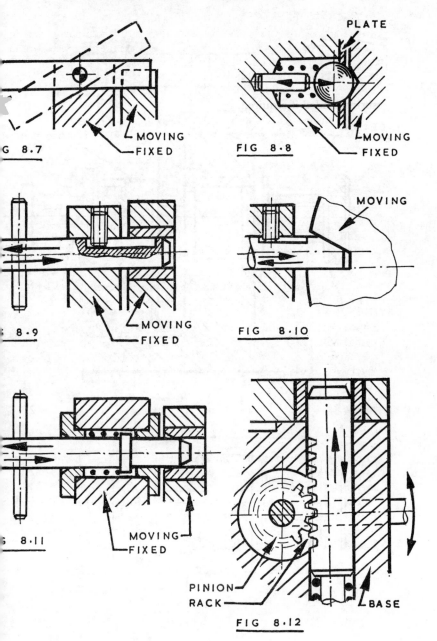

PLATE

MOVING
FIXED
G 8.7

FIG 8·8
MOVING
FIXED

MOVING
8·9
MOVING
FIXED

FIG 8·10

MOVING
FIXED
8·11

PINION
RACK
BASE

FIG 8·12

67

INDEXING DRILL JIG

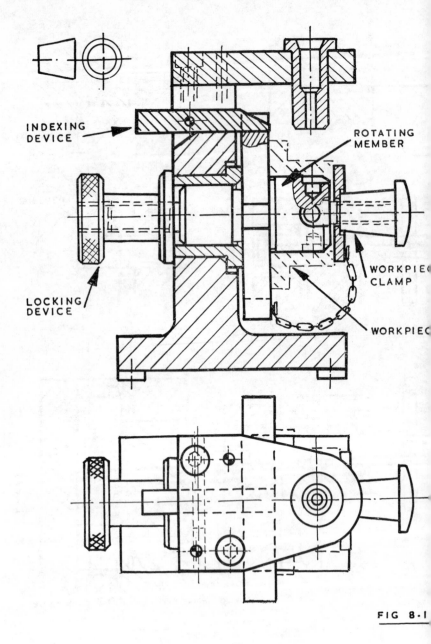

INDEXING
DEVICE

ROTATING
MEMBER

WORKPIEC
CLAMP

LOCKING
DEVICE

WORKPIEC

FIG 8·1

68

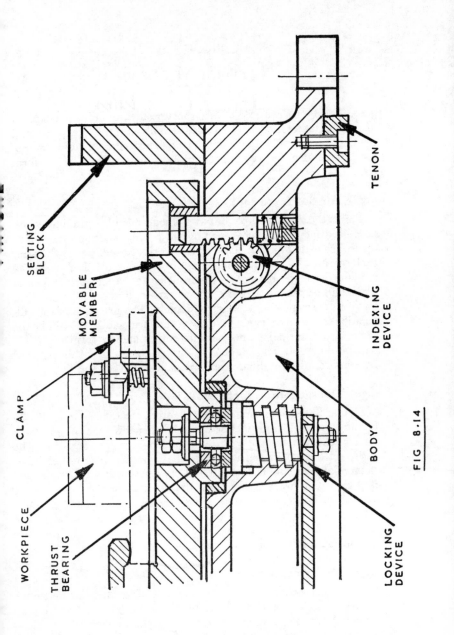

WORKPIECE

CLAMP

MOVABLE
MEMBER

SETTING
BLOCK

THRUST
BEARING

INDEXING
DEVICE

BODY

TENON

LOCKING
DEVICE

FIG 8.14

CHAPTER 9

FORM TOOLS

9.10. Form tools are used to turn short profiles, usually on a capstan or a turret lathe; the form tool is fed radially into the workpiece, and the depth is controlled by a depth stop. The main types of form tool are: 1, Flat form tool; 2, Tangential form tool; and 3, Circular form tool.

9.20. The flat form tool

This is the simplest type, but as it is sharpened by grinding its top face (see page 71) it is weakened by sharpening, and must be packed up to bring its top face back to the workpiece centre height after each regrind. When manufacturing this type of tool it is necessary to consider its shape normal to the front face; the tool profile in this plane will be similar to that of the workpiece, but modified to allow for front clearance angle, and rake angle. The principle of the calculation is shown on pages 71 and 72; the form width 'W' will be the same in the normal plane, but the corresponding form depth 'T' will be different. The shape of a curved form can be determined by considering co-ordinate dimensions such as 'W' and 'T'.

9.30. The tangential form tool

Similar to the flat form tool, but the front clearance is obtained by holding the tool in an inclined tool holder; this type of tool has a longer life than the flat form tool due to its shape, and it can be easily set so that its top face is at the workpiece centre height. A tangential form tool is illustrated in fig. 9.2, and it will be seen that if a zero rake angle is required, the top face of the tool must be ground to an angle equal to the clearance angle; if a rake angle other than zero is required, the clearance angle must be taken into account. The shape of the tool in the plane normal to the front face is calculated in the same way as for the flat form tool.

9.40. The circular form tool

Used very extensively on single spindle automatic bar machines, where it is held in a holder from the cross slide. The tool centre must be set above that of the workpiece, to produce a clearance angle so that the tool does not rub on the workpiece. The 'outside diameter'

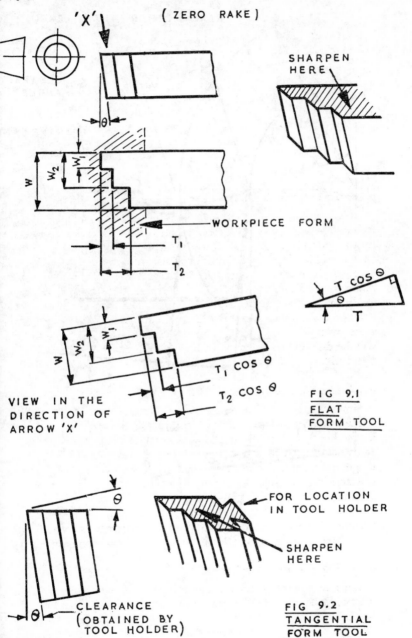

VIEW IN THE
DIRECTION OF
ARROW 'X'

WORKPIECE FORM

FIG 9.1
FLAT
FORM TOOL

FOR LOCATION
IN TOOL HOLDER

SHARPEN
HERE

CLEARANCE
(OBTAINED BY
TOOL HOLDER)

FIG 9.2
TANGENTIAL
FORM TOOL

FORM TOOLS - FLAT & TANGENTIAL

(RAKE OTHER THAN ZERO)

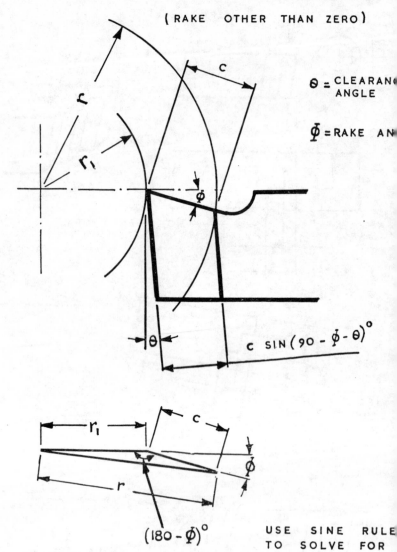

θ = CLEARANCE ANGLE

ϕ = RAKE ANGLE

$c \sin(90 - \phi - \theta)^{\circ}$

$(180 - \phi)^{\circ}$

USE SINE RULE TO SOLVE FOR

FIG 9.3

CIRCULAR FORM TOOL

(ZERO RAKE)

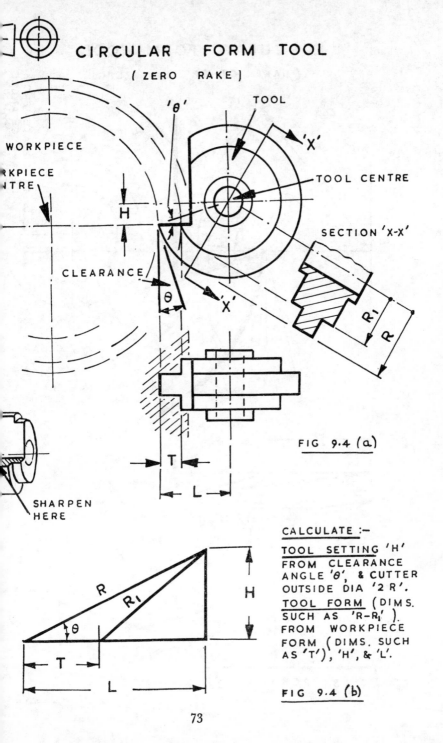

WORKPIECE

WORKPIECE CENTRE

'θ'

TOOL

'X'

TOOL CENTRE

SECTION 'X-X'

H

CLEARANCE

θ

'X'

R_1

R

SHARPEN HERE

T

L

FIG 9.4 (a)

R

R_1

θ

T

L

H

<u>CALCULATE :-</u>

TOOL SETTING 'H' FROM CLEARANCE ANGLE 'θ', & CUTTER OUTSIDE DIA '2 R'.
TOOL FORM (DIMS. SUCH AS 'R-R_1').
FROM WORKPIECE FORM (DIMS. SUCH AS 'T'), 'H', & 'L'.

FIG 9.4 (b)

CIRCULAR FORM TOOL
(RAKE OTHER THAN ZERO)

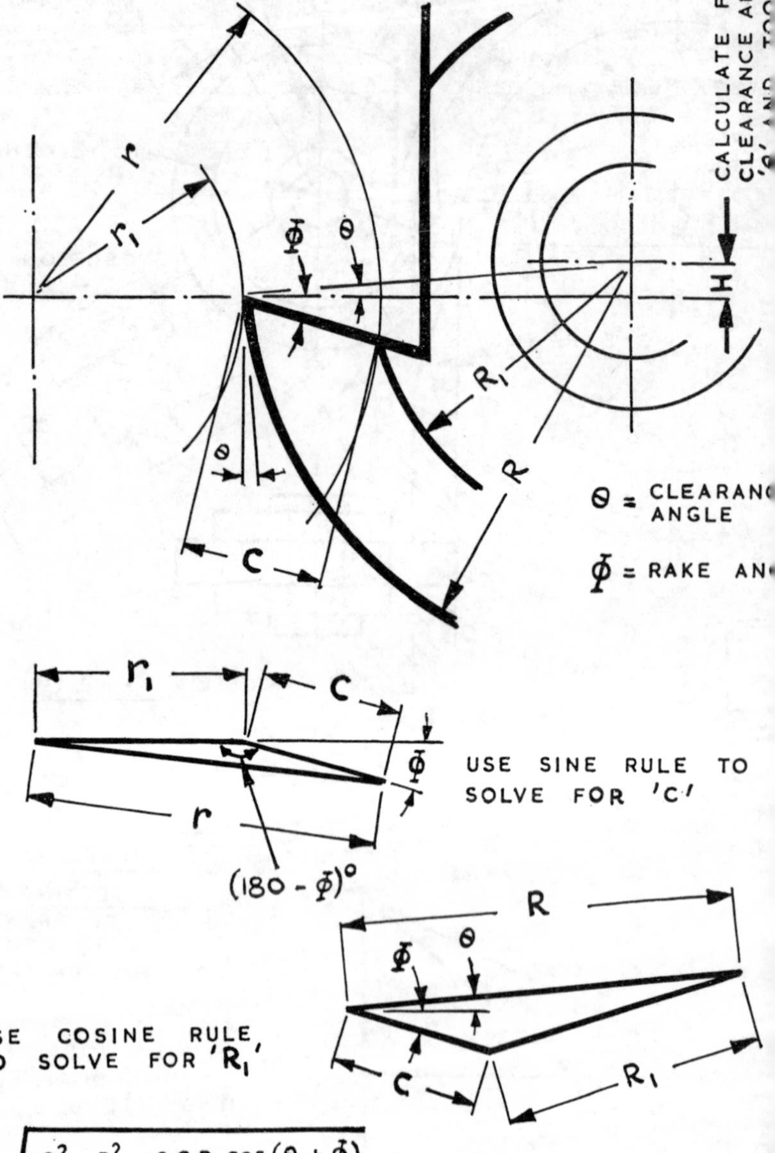

CALCULATE FROM CLEARANCE ANGLE 'θ' AND TOOL

Θ = CLEARANCE ANGLE

ϕ = RAKE ANGLE

USE SINE RULE TO SOLVE FOR 'C'

$(180 - \phi)°$

USE COSINE RULE TO SOLVE FOR 'R₁'

$$R_1 = \sqrt{C^2 + R^2 - 2C.R\cos(\theta + \phi)}$$

FIG 9.5

74

of the tool is between 50 and 125 mm, and must be taken into account when calculating the tool centre height 'H' (see page 73). The cutter blank is first made to the required radial shape and then gashed to produce the top cutting face; it is therefore necessary to give details of the tool shape as radial dimensions such as $R — R_1$ (see pages 73 and 74). The tool is sharpened by grinding the 'top face', and rotated about its axis to bring the tool to the workpiece centre height; this type of tool has a long life, and will continue to give service over about 270° of rotation as a result of regrinding.

9.50. Calculations for form tools

The differences between the workpiece shape and the form tool shape will be very small, demanding accurate calculations. The accuracy obtained using a calculator is usually adequate, but when mathematical tables are used they should be at least five-figure tables.

When the difference between the workpiece dimensions and those of the form tool is small compared with the workpiece tolerances, the tool can be made to the workpiece dimensions. This is important when the 'corrected' tool profile is more difficult to produce than the workpiece profile (for example, when the workpiece profile is made up of circular arcs).

CHAPTER 10

LIMIT GAUGES

10.10. When dimensioning a component it is necessary to stipulate the permitted variation in its size because errors will occur owing to inaccuracies in the machine tools, jigs and fixtures, measurement, etc. The extremes of size that are permitted are called the **limits of size** (or more simply the 'limits'), and the difference between these limits is called the **variation tolerated** (or more simply the 'tolerance'). The tolerances should be as large as possible to minimise the cost of the component, but be sufficiently small to ensure that the required fit, or the degree of interchangeability between parts, is ensured.

10.11. The limit that is associated with the greatest amount of metal is often called the **maximum metal limit,** and that associated with the least amount of metal is often called the **minimum metal limit**. The largest shaft size permitted is the maximum metal limit, and the smallest shaft size permitted is the minimum metal limit; similarly, the largest hole size permitted is the minimum metal limit, and the smallest hole size permitted is the maximum metal limit.

10.12. One method of inspecting parts is to use limit gauges; these gauges are designed to accept the workpiece if its size and shape lies within the specified limits. A limit gauge (or pair of limit gauges) consists of a 'GO' member that will pass over or through a correct feature, and a 'NOT GO' member that will not pass over or through a correct feature. The 'GO' member checks the maximum metal limit, and the 'NOT GO' member checks the minimum metal limit. The main disadvantages associated with the use of limit gauges is that the extent of error is not indicated when a workpiece is rejected, and that the system imposes smaller tolerances than stipulated on the drawing of the workpiece to allow for tolerances when the gauge is manufactured and also for gauge wear.

10.20. The Taylor principle (stated in 1905 by William Taylor, of Messrs Taylor, Taylor, and Hobson).

As stated above, the 'GO' member is used to check the maximum metal limit, which in turn controls the shape of the workpiece; the 'GO' member must be full form, because, as shown in fig. 10.3, a 'GO' member that is not full form, will accept an incorrectly-shaped

76

workpiece. Taylor stated that **the 'GO' gauge should incorporate the maximum metal limits of as many dimensions as it is convenient and suitable to check in one operation.**

Taylor also stated that **the 'NOT GO' gauges should be separate, and check the minimum metal limit of each dimension in turn;** this is because, as shown in fig. 10.4, if more than one dimension is checked at a time by the 'NOT GO' member, it will enter, not enter, or pass over the feature as long as ONE dimension is within limits, and can therefore accept an incorrect workpiece.

10.30. Limit gauge tolerances

It is necessary to allow manufacturing tolerances when designing a gauge, but it is also necessary that these tolerances do not permit inaccurate parts to be passed by the gauge, or excessively reduce the workpiece tolerances. British Standard B.S. 969, Plain Limit Gauges —Limits and Tolerances, recommends that the limits on the 'GO' gauge are such that its size is **within** the limits of size for the workpiece, and that the limits on the 'NOT GO' are such that its size is **outside** the limits of size for the workpiece. When made to these limits the 'NOT GO' will not accept faulty parts, but the 'GO' will reject parts that are close to the maximum metal limits; the latter condition will rarely occur in practice. The gauge tolerance is usually one-tenth of the workpiece tolerance.

10.40. Allowance for gauge wear

B.S. 969 recommends that where the workpiece tolerance exceeds about 0·1 mm additional metal be left on the 'GO' gauge surface to allow for wear (this has the effect of placing the manufacturing limits for the 'GO' gauge still further within the workpiece limits). The standard also recommends that if the workpiece tolerance is too small to permit this, the gauge should be made from a specially hard-wearing material.

10.50. Materials for limit gauges

Gauges are usually made from case-hardening steel that is heat-treated during the manufacture of the gauge, or from cast steel (with between about 0·7 and 1·2% carbon) that is usually hardened, but may be hard enough 'as received'. Larger gauges are sometimes made from grey cast iron, or steel that is chromium plated to increase its wear resistance.

THE TAYLOR PRINCIPLE

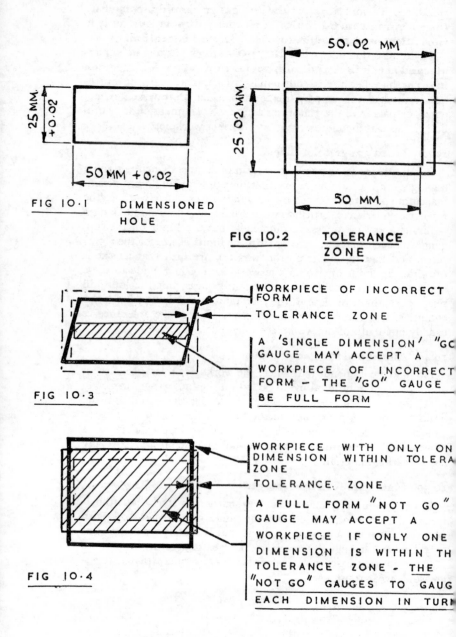

FIG 10·1 DIMENSIONED HOLE

FIG 10·2 TOLERANCE ZONE

FIG 10·3

WORKPIECE OF INCORRECT FORM

TOLERANCE ZONE

A 'SINGLE DIMENSION' "GO" GAUGE MAY ACCEPT A WORKPIECE OF INCORRECT FORM — THE "GO" GAUGE BE FULL FORM

FIG 10·4

WORKPIECE WITH ONLY ON DIMENSION WITHIN TOLERA ZONE

TOLERANCE ZONE

A FULL FORM "NOT GO" GAUGE MAY ACCEPT A WORKPIECE IF ONLY ONE DIMENSION IS WITHIN TH TOLERANCE ZONE — THE "NOT GO" GAUGES TO GAUG EACH DIMENSION IN TURN

Design of limit gauges

10.60. Plain plug gauges (used to gauge cylindrical holes)

In order to completely satisfy Taylor's principle, the 'GO' end should be full form, and be the same length as the hole to be gauged; it is often inconvenient to make the 'GO' end the same length as the hole, but except when large holes are gauged, it is full form. When large holes are gauged the gauge members are of the the 'bar' type to reduce the weight of the gauge; this type of gauge does not satisfy Taylor's principle because it only checks across the diameter.

Similarly, the 'NOT GO' end should be diamond-shaped so that it only checks across the diameter. Sometimes the 'NOT GO' end is flatted, and it then partly satisfies Taylor's principle; large gauges of the 'bar' type also partly satisfy Taylor's principle.

The gauging members may be integral with the handle (a 'solid' gauge) or the gauging members made separately and engaged together to form an assembly (a 'renewable end' gauge). B.S. 1044: 1964, Gauge Blanks, does not include 'solid' gauges because it is now common practice to use renewable end gauges with a light alloy or plastics handle. Renewable end gauges can be collet type, taper-lock type, trilock type or 'bar' type. The 'GO' and 'NOT GO' members may have separate handles, be at opposite ends of one handle, or combined as one gauging member of the progressive gauge type (see page 81).

The ends of large plug gauges should be protected from becoming burred when placed on a machine table, by providing a 'guard extension' (as shown in fig. 10.5); this should be applied to gauges

FIG 10·5

of more than about 75 mm diameter excepting those for testing blind holes to their full depth.

The centres should be good quality, they should not be large, and the length of the cone should be kept short. The mouth of the centre should be protected by a small recess 1 mm or 2 mm deep (see fig. 10.6).

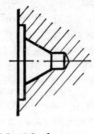

FIG 10·6

Adequate air venting should be provided when small gauges are used for blind holes; when a gauge is more than 100 mm dia. lightening holes are incorporated, which also give the required air venting. The marking of gauges should be kept to a minimum; the marking should include the limiting dimension controlled by the gauge, 'GO' or 'NOT GO' (alternatively 'H' or 'L'—high limit or low limit), 'General' or 'Reference', the manufacturer's name or trade mark, and the gauge serial number.

Some typical plug gauges are illustrated on page 81.

GAP (OR SNAP) GAUGES—USED TO GAUGE SHAFTS

10.61. In order to fully satisfy Taylor's principle, a shaft should be checked by a full form ring 'GO' gauge, and a gap-type 'NOT-GO' gauge. In practice it is found to be more convenient to use 'GO' and 'NOT GO' gap gauges for size gauging, and to use other gauges for shape if required.

The gap gauge can be double ended, or be progressive; a progressive gap gauge is shown in fig. 10.11. Adjustable gap gauges are used very frequently; these gauges have screw-adjusted anvils that are locked in position, and the locking-screw holes sealed with lead or wax. These adjustable gauges may have four adjustable anvils (fig. 10.12(a)) or two adjustable anvils and one fixed anvil (fig. 10.12(b)).

GAUGING OF SCREW THREADS

10.62. External screw threads are usually gauged with a plain gap gauge for the major (outside) diameter, and a thread gauge for the effective diameter (the effective diameter is the diameter of an imaginary cylinder whose generator cuts the thread such that the

LIMIT GAUGES

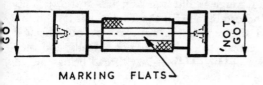

FIG 10.7
DOUBLE END

MARKING FLATS

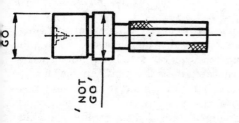

FIG 10.8
PROGRESSIVE TYPE

'NOT GO'

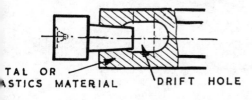

FIG 10.9
TAPER-LOCK
RENEWABLE-END
TYPE

TAL OR
ASTICS MATERIAL

DRIFT HOLE

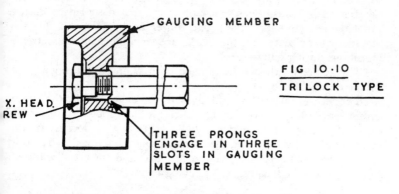

GAUGING MEMBER

FIG 10.10
TRILOCK TYPE

X. HEAD.
REW

THREE PRONGS
ENGAGE IN THREE
SLOTS IN GAUGING
MEMBER

FIGS 10.7 - 10.10   PLAIN PLUG GAUGES

distance between the points where it cuts the flanks of the thread groove, is equal to half the pitch of the thread).

The 'Matrix' thread gauge is illustrated in fig. 10.13(a). This gauge has two sets of adjustable anvils; the front anvils form a full form 'GO' gauge, and the rear anvils form a 'NOT GO' effective diameter gauge. The rear anvils gauge only two threads, and they are shaped so that error of pitch of the screw thread being gauged will not interfere with their function. Both the front and the rear anvils are shaped so that the helix angle of the thread being gauged will not cause interference. The 'GO' and 'NOT GO' anvils are shown in figs. 10.13(b) and 10.13(c).

Internal screw threads are usually gauged with a plain plug gauge for the minor (inside) diameter, and a double-ended screw plug gauge for the effective diameter. The 'GO' member is full form, but the 'NOT GO' member has truncated threads so that only the effective diameter is gauged. It is common to have a dirt clearance groove cut axial to the thread to a depth slightly below the root of the thread. The general design notes already given regarding plain plug gauges also apply to screw plug gauges.

THICKNESS AND LENGTH GAUGES

10.63. Gauges for thickness are shown in figs. 10.15, and a typical length gauge is shown in fig. 10.16. These gauges are made from gauge plate, and may be double-ended or single-ended.

RECESS GAUGES

10.64. Fig. 10.17 shows a plate gauge for checking the recess depth; care must be taken when this type of gauge is designed, to ensure that the leading end of the gauge will enter the hole, and that the gauge will be seated on the workpiece face, when in the extreme positions during gauging.

The recess width can be gauged with a simple plate gauge as shown in fig. 10.18.

The recess diameter is more difficult to gauge because the gauge must enter the small diameter hole before gauging the recess diameter. Fig. 10.19 shows a typical gauge that locates in the smaller diameter hole, and the recess diameter is gauged by rotating the lobed member; the position for 'GO' and 'NOT GO' must be indicated on the locating and gauging members.

STEP GAUGES

10.65. These gauges are designed so that the workpiece is accepted if one step is below the datum face, and the other step is above the datum face; they are convenient to use if the step is at least 0·2 mm.

LIMIT GAUGES

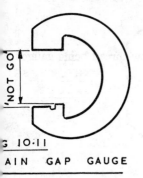

G 10·11

AIN GAP GAUGE

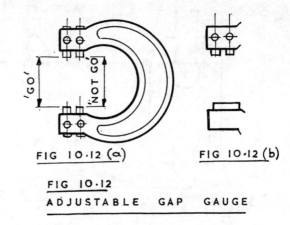

FIG 10·12 (a)

FIG 10·12 (b)

FIG 10·12
ADJUSTABLE GAP GAUGE

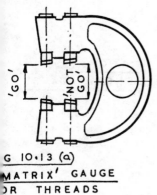

G 10·13 (a)

MATRIX' GAUGE

OR THREADS

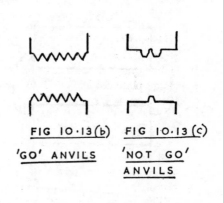

FIG 10·13(b)   FIG 10·13(c)

'GO' ANVILS   'NOT GO'
ANVILS

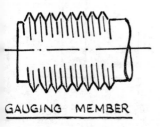

GAUGING MEMBER

FIG 10·14

SCREW PLUG GAUGE

LIMIT GAUGES

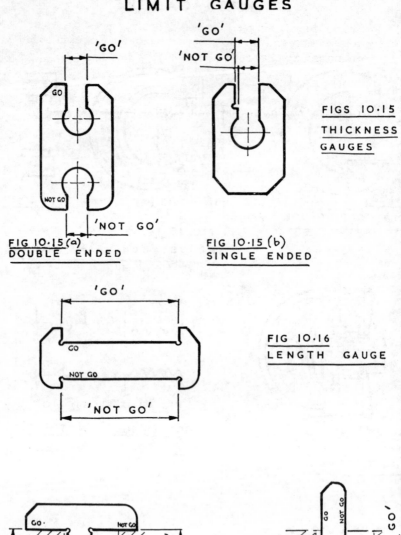

'GO'
'NOT GO'

FIG 10.15 (a)
DOUBLE ENDED

'GO'
'NOT GO'

FIG 10.15 (b)
SINGLE ENDED

FIGS 10.15
THICKNESS
GAUGES

'GO'
GO
NOT GO
'NOT GO'

FIG 10.16
LENGTH GAUGE

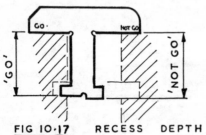

GO
NOT GO
'GO'
'NOT GO'

FIG 10.17   RECESS DEPTH

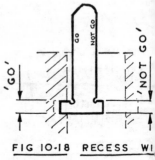

GO
NOT GO
'GO'
'NOT GO'

FIG 10.18   RECESS WI

84

Fig. 10.20 shows a simple stepped-pin depth gauge. Fig. 10.21 shows a taper plug, and fig. 10.22 shows a taper ring gauge; in both these examples the datum face is the workpiece face.

POSITION AND RECEIVER GAUGES

10.66. Position gauges are used to check the relative position of several features (see fig. 10.23), and receiver gauges are used to check several features simultaneously.

REFERENCES

B.S. 4500: 1969. ISO Limits and Fits.
B.S. 1044: Part 1: 1964. Specification for Gauge Blanks.
B.S. 969: 1953. Plain Limit Gauges—Limits and Tolerances.
B.S. 919: Part 3: 1968. Gauges for ISO Metric Screw Threads.

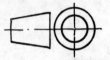

LIMIT GAUGES

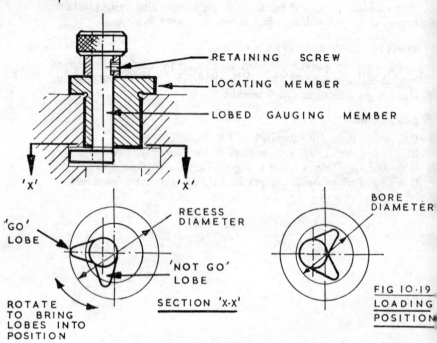

RETAINING SCREW

LOCATING MEMBER

LOBED GAUGING MEMBER

'X'   'X'

'GO' LOBE

RECESS DIAMETER

'NOT GO' LOBE

ROTATE TO BRING LOBES INTO POSITION

SECTION 'X-X'

BORE DIAMETER

FIG 10·19 LOADING POSITION

FIG 10·19   RECESS DIAMETER GAUGE

TOLERANCE

RETAINING SCREW

LOCATING MEMBER

STEPPED PIN

DEPTH

FIG 10·20
STEPPED-PIN DEPTH GAUGE

86

LIMIT GAUGES

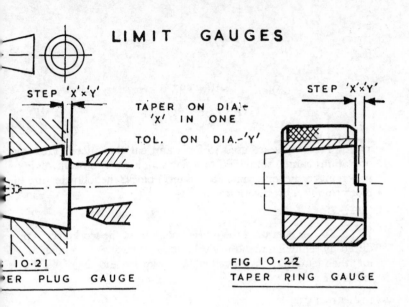

STEP 'X' x 'Y'

TAPER ON DIA.-
'X' IN ONE

TOL. ON DIA.-'Y'

STEP 'X' x 'Y'

FIG 10·21
TAPER PLUG GAUGE

FIG 10·22
TAPER RING GAUGE

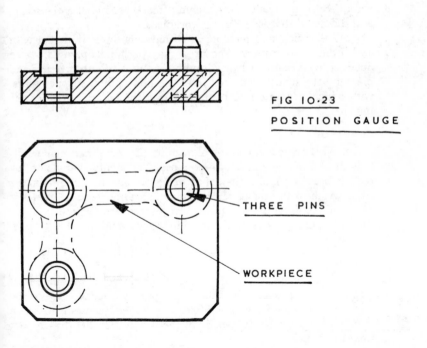

FIG 10·23
POSITION GAUGE

THREE PINS

WORKPIECE

87

CHAPTER 11

PRESS TOOLS

11.10. Press tools are used to form and cut thin metal. Press tool operations can be simplified to a few simple operations involving a punch and a die, or a punch and a form block; the following are the more common presswork operations:

BLANKING

11.11. In this operation the outside contour of the workpiece is produced by removing metal from the strip by means of a punch and a die; the metal that is removed is the workpiece and the metal that is left is the scrap.

PIERCING

11.12. This is the cutting of holes within the outside contour of the workpiece by a punch; the punching (metal removed) is the scrap, and the metal that is left is the workpiece.

11.121. Blanking and piercing are often done in conjunction with each other in one press. The press may be hand operated, or be operated by a crank or by hydraulic pressure. In both piercing and blanking the strip is removed from the punch by a stripper plate, with which it comes into contact during the return stroke of the punch.

BENDING

11.13. This operation consists of forming the metal between a suitably shaped punch and a forming block. The included angle on the tools is usually smaller than that to be produced to allow for the spring-back of the metal after forming. Bending of large plates is usually done using a brake press; this press is fitted with a brake so that the operator can stop the machine very rapidly, and also 'inch' if necessary.

DRAWING

11.14. Cups, shells and similar parts are produced by pushing metal through a die so that it assumes the shape of the space between the punch and the die. The spring-back of the metal causes it to foul a stripping edge on the underside of the die, to free the drawn part from the punch.

Some typical press-tool sets are illustrated on pages 90–95.

SIMPLE BLANKING SET (see fig. 11.1 on page 90)

11.20. In this set the die (or blanking bed) is made of casehardened steel, or of alloy steel that is hardened and tempered; it is held in a cast iron bolster. The metal is removed by a punch that is made of hardened and tempered cast steel or alloy steel. The stock is positioned under the punch with the aid of a guide and a stop; the stock is positioned by locating the hole made by the previous blanking, against the stop. The remaining stock is removed from the punch by the stripper plate; a window is cut in the stripper plate so that the stop can be seen by the operator.

BLANKING AND PIERCING TOOL SET (see fig. 11.2 on page 91)

11.30. The set illustrated is for the production of washers, and is of the follow-on type. The hole is first pierced by tool '1', and then the stock is positioned under tool '2', which blanks the washer; one washer is completed at each stroke of the press. The hole left by the blanking operation is used to position the stock against the spring-loaded stop, the top plate is located relative to the bottom plate by guide posts, and the blanking punch is provided with a pilot to locate it relative to the pierced hole. The punches are held in the top plate as shown in the illustration.

11.31. In order to reduce the load on the press, the punch or the die is given an 'angle of shear' (see figs. 11.3 and 11.4 on page 93) to cause a gradual shearing of the metal; this introduces a side thrust that can, however, be nullified by having a double shear angle.

11.32. The forces caused by the punching and by the stripping operations when several punches are involved can be reduced by making the punches of different lengths so that they do not all engage the workpiece at the same time.

11.33. When blanking and piercing operations are done, the metal is fractured on both sides; there must be a clearance between the punch and the die to ensure that these two fractures meet and so produce a clean edge. The amount of clearance depends upon the thickness of the metal to be sheared, and its mechanical properties; the clearance is usually about $\frac{1}{20}$ of the thickness of the metal. When blanking, the die is made the size of the workpiece and the punch made smaller to allow the clearance; when piercing, the punch is made the workpiece-hole size, and the die is made oversized for clearance.

11.34. After blanking or piercing, the metal that is removed must drop easily through the die; this is made easier by introducing an angular clearance in the die. The die is resharpened by grinding its

D

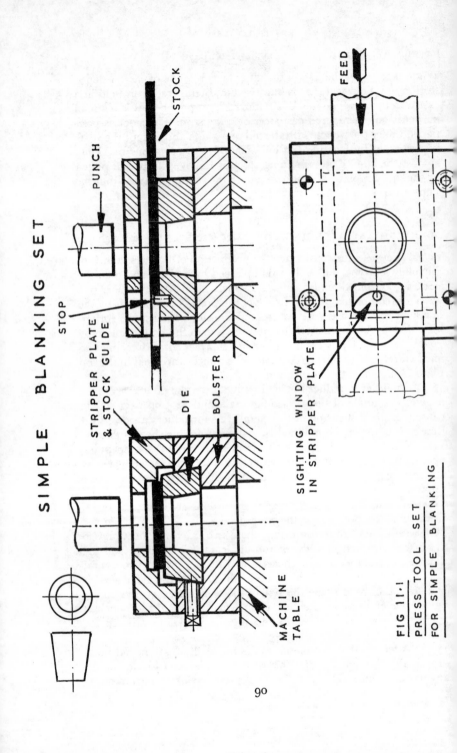

SIMPLE BLANKING SET

STOCK

PUNCH

STOP

STRIPPER PLATE & STOCK GUIDE

DIE

BOLSTER

MACHINE TABLE

FEED

SIGHTING WINDOW IN STRIPPER PLATE

FIG 11·1
PRESS TOOL SET
FOR SIMPLE BLANKING

90

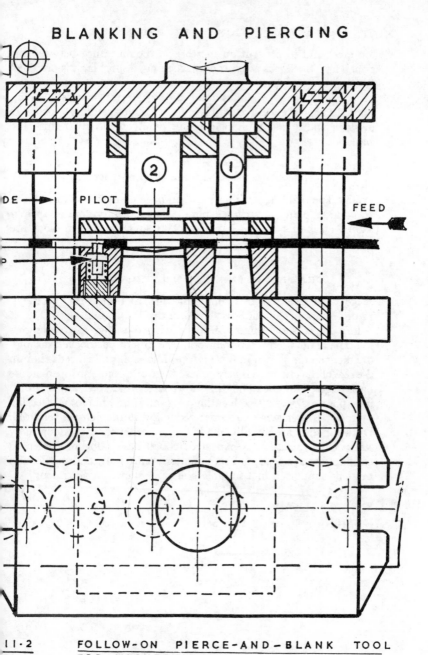

DE →

PILOT →

FEED →

② ①

11·2   FOLLOW-ON PIERCE-AND-BLANK TOOL FOR WASHERS

top face, and to prevent an increase in the clearance between the punch and the die as a result of sharpening, a short land is provided (see fig. 11.5).

11.35. The layout of blanks along the stock must be carefully considered to avoid excessive wastage; fig. 11.6 illustrates how a change in stock width and a change in the arrangement can reduce the wastage.

BENDING (see figs. 11.7 and 11.8 on page 94)

11.40. The bending sets illustrated on page 94 include a form block and guide plate; a stripper plate is unnecessary, but a spring-loaded ejection system is included. The punch and form block are made from hardened steel.

DRAWING (see figs. 11.9 and 11.10 on page 95)

11.50. The essentials of a simple drawing tool set are shown in fig. 11.9; a stripping shoulder is shown in this illustration.

Figs. 11.10 show some typical drawing dies; fig. 11.10(*a*) shows the type of die used when the workpiece cannot be knocked through the die; the die shown in fig. 11.10(*b*) allows a gradual reduction in the size of the cup, and is used where the workpiece is stripped on the back edge of the die. The dies shown in figs. 11.10(*c*) and 11.10(*d*) incorporate a workpiece locating ring, and the double die (see fig. 11.10(*e*)) is used where a larger reduction in diameter is required. Drawing dies are usually made from hardened carbon or alloy steel; when abrasion is expected, cobalt-base alloy or cemented carbide dies are used, but these materials are hard and brittle and must be supported in a suitable holder, as shown in fig. 11.10(*f*).

REFERENCE

B.S. 1609: 1949. Press Tool Sets.

BLANKING AND PIERCING

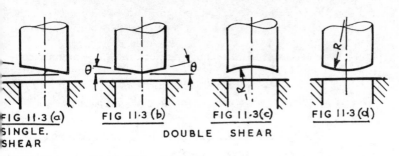

FIG 11·3 (a)
SINGLE.
SHEAR

θ   θ
FIG 11·3 (b)   FIG 11·3(c)   FIG 11·3 (d)
DOUBLE   SHEAR

FIG 11·3   SHEAR   ON   PUNCH

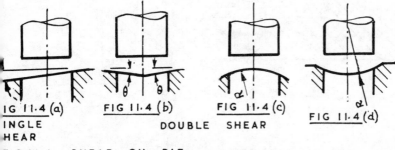

IG 11·4 (a)   FIG 11·4 (b)   FIG 11·4 (c)   FIG 11·4 (d)
INGLE   θ   θ   α
HEAR   DOUBLE   SHEAR

FIG 11·4   SHEAR   ON   DIE

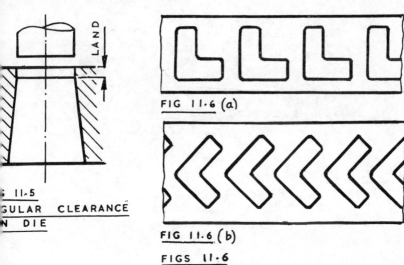

LAND

11·5
GULAR   CLEARANCE
N DIE

FIG 11·6 (a)

FIG 11·6 (b)

FIGS 11·6
BLANKING   LAYOUTS

93

BENDING

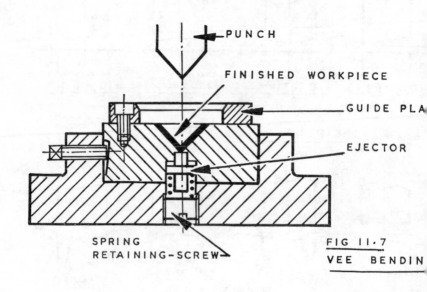

FIG 11·7
VEE BENDIN

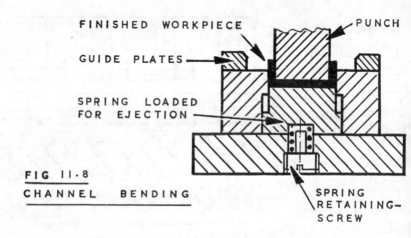

FIG 11·8
CHANNEL BENDING

94

DRAWING

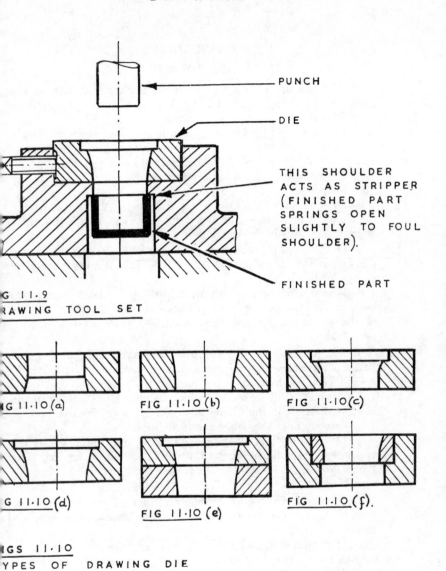

PUNCH

DIE

THIS SHOULDER
ACTS AS STRIPPER
(FINISHED PART
SPRINGS OPEN
SLIGHTLY TO FOUL
SHOULDER).

FINISHED PART

FIG 11.9
DRAWING TOOL SET

FIG 11.10 (a)

FIG 11.10 (b)

FIG 11.10 (c)

FIG 11.10 (d)

FIG 11.10 (e)

FIG 11.10 (f).

FIGS 11.10
TYPES OF DRAWING DIE

95

EXERCISES

1. Design a drill jig for use when drilling the four holes in the flange of the Housing shown in fig. E.1. The Housing is complete except for these holes.

2. Design a drill jig for use when drilling and reaming the six holes in the flange of the Adaptor shown in fig. E.2. The Adaptor is complete except for these holes and the hole in the shank.

3. Design a drill stop assembly and setting gauge for use in the above operation.

4. Design a drill jig for use when drilling the 12 mm dia. hole in the shank of the Adaptor shown in fig. E.2. This hole is machined after the six holes in the flange (see exercise 2 above).

5. Design a simple solid-type jig for use when drilling the 10 mm dia. hole in the stem of the Pin shown in fig. E.3. The Pin is complete except for this hole.

6. Design a drill jig for use when drilling the four 10 mm dia. holes in the square flange of the Elbow shown in fig. E.4. The face of the square flange has been machined prior to this drilling operation.

7. Design a milling fixture for use when machining the elongated flange of the Elbow shown in fig. E.4. This operation is done directly after drilling the four holes (see exercise 6).

8. Design a drill jig for use when drilling the two holes in the elongated flange of the Elbow shown in fig. E.4. This operation is done directly after the flange is milled (see exercise 7).

9. Design a drill jig for use when drilling and counterboring the two holes in the flange of the Connection shown in fig. E.5. The flange face and the bore of this part have been machined before this operation.

10. Design a drill jig for drilling and spotfacing the 25 mm dia. boss of the Connection shown in fig. E.5. This is done after the flange is drilled.

11. Design a drill jig for use when drilling the 2 mm dia. in the stem of the Special Bolt shown in fig. 2.1 (on page 8). The hole is drilled at operation 7 (see the operation layout on page 8).

12. Design a drill jig for use when drilling and spotfacing the four holes in the flange of the Fulcrum Pin shown in fig. 2.2 (page 11). These holes are drilled at operation 3 (see operation layout on page 10).

DIMS IN MM.

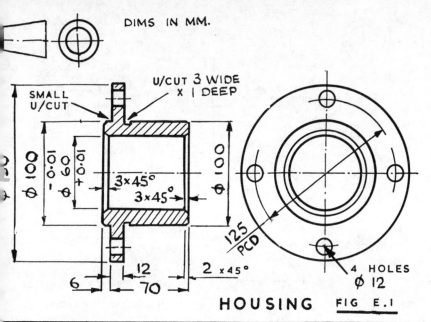

HOUSING FIG E.1

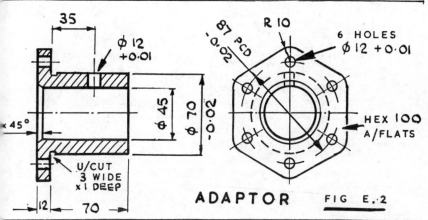

ADAPTOR FIG E.2

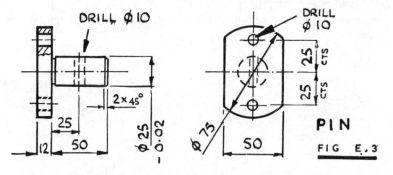

PIN FIG E.3

97

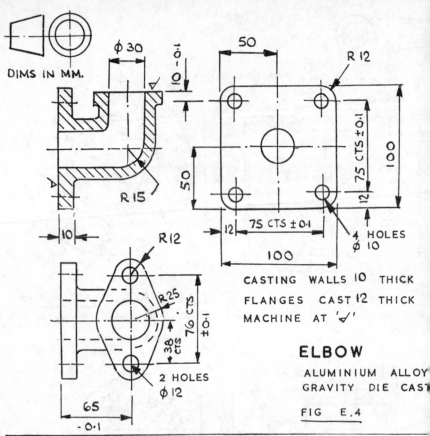

DIMS IN MM.

CASTING WALLS 10 THICK
FLANGES CAST 12 THICK
MACHINE AT '√'

ELBOW

ALUMINIUM ALLOY
GRAVITY DIE CAST

FIG E.4

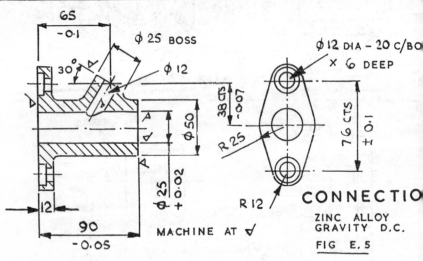

MACHINE AT √

CONNECTIO

ZINC ALLOY
GRAVITY D.C.
FIG E.5

98

13. Design a drill jig for use when drilling the two 3 mm dia. holes in the stem of the Fulcrum Pin shown in fig. 2.2. (page 11). These holes are drilled at operation 7 (see page 10).

14. Design a milling fixture for use when milling the 6 mm slot in the Base shown in fig. E.6. This is the last machining operation to be done on the Base. Details of the milling machine table are given in the fig.

15. Design an index drilling jig for use when machining four 12 mm dia. holes in the Boss shown in fig. E.7. The Boss is complete except for these holes.

16. Design an index milling fixture for use when milling the 6 mm wide slots in the Cover shown in fig. E.8. The Cover is complete except for these slots. One slot is to be produced right across the component, the fixture indexed through 90° and the second slot milled right across. The milling machine table is as shown in fig. E.6.

17. Design a string milling fixture to gang mill the flats and the slot in the head of the Special Bolt shown in fig. 2.1 (page 8), at operation 4 (see also page 8). Ten workpieces are to be milled at a time, and the milling machine table is as for exercise 16 above.

18. Design a turning fixture for use when turning the stem of the Fulcrum Pin shown in fig. 2.2 (page 11). This is done at operation 5 (see page 10); the lathe spindle nose is as shown in fig. E.9.

19. Design a turning fixture for use when machining the 38 mm dia. bore in the Bearing Bracket shown in fig. E.9. The Bearing Bracket is complete except for this machining, and the lathe spindle nose is as illustrated.

20. Design a press tool set for blanking and piercing the Bell Crank shown in fig. E.10 from 2 mm thick mild steel.

21. Design (i) a blanking and piercing press tool set to produce the Bracket shown in fig. 11, before bending, and (ii) a bending tool set for bending the Bracket.

22. Design the following limit gauges:

(i) A plug gauge for the 12 mm dia. holes in the flange of the Adaptor (fig. E.2).

(ii) A plug gauge for the 60 mm dia. bore of the Housing (fig. E.1).

(iii) A gap gauge for the 70 mm dia. stem of the Adaptor (fig. E.2).

23. Fig. E.12 (page 102) gives details of a vee groove to be turned using a form tool.

(a) Draw and dimension a flat form tool to produce the groove; the tool is to have a 5° front clearance angle, and zero rake angle.

(b) Draw and dimension a flat form tool to produce the groove;

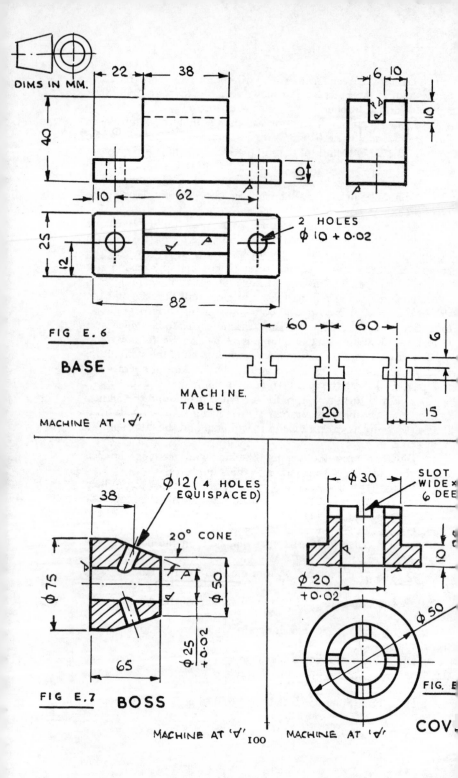

DIMS IN MM.

FIG E.6

BASE

MACHINE AT '√'

MACHINE. TABLE

FIG E.7 BOSS

2 HOLES
φ 10 + 0.02

φ 12 (4 HOLES
EQUISPACED)

20° CONE

MACHINE AT '√' 100

SLOT
WIDE ×
6 DEE

φ 30

φ 20
+0.02

φ 50

FIG. E

COV.

MACHINE AT '√'

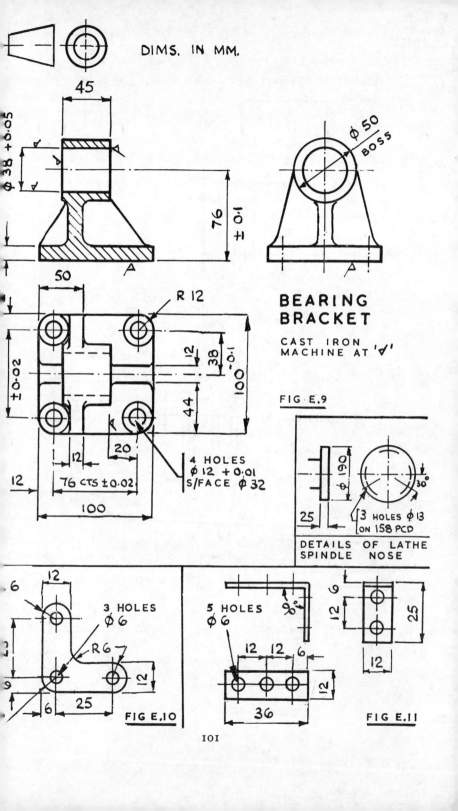

DIMS. IN MM.

45

$\phi 38 + 0.05$

76 ± 0.1

50

A

$\phi 50$ BOSS

BEARING BRACKET

CAST IRON
MACHINE AT '∀'

FIG. E.9

50

R 12

12

38 - 0.1

100

44

±1 ±0.02

12

20

76 CTS ±0.02

100

12

4 HOLES
$\phi 12 + 0.01$
S/FACE $\phi 32$

$\phi 160$

25

3 HOLES $\phi 13$
ON 158 PCD

30°

DETAILS OF LATHE
SPINDLE NOSE

12

6

3 HOLES
$\phi 6$

R6

12

6

25

FIG E.10

5 HOLES
$\phi 6$

90°

12 12 6

36

12

6

12

25

12

FIG E.11

101

this tool to have a 5° front clearance angle, and a 10° front rake angle.

24. Fig. E.13 gives details of a stepped groove to be turned using a circular form tool.

(a) Draw and dimension a circular form tool to produce this groove; this tool to have a 5° front clearance angle, and a zero rake

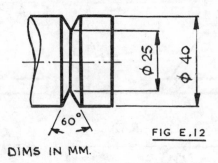

FIG E.12

DIMS IN MM.

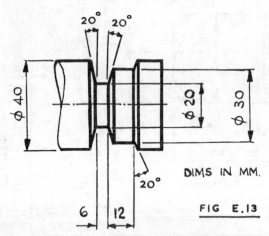

DIMS IN MM.

FIG E.13

angle. Calculate also the height of the tool centre above that of the workpiece.

(b) Draw and dimension a circular form tool to produce the groove; this tool to have a 6° front clearance angle, and a 15° front rake angle.

INDEX